Praise for
Lovin' with Grit and Grace

"Jess Ronne is one of the most inspiring human beings on planet earth, and her story will forever change your perspective in positive and practical ways. This book isn't just an incredible marriage resource; it's an irresistible invitation to embrace all aspects of life with more grit and grace."

—**Dave Willis,** coauthor of *The Naked Marriage* and cohost of *The Naked Marriage* podcast

"Once again, author Jess Ronne pierces readers' hearts and provides practical insights! In *Lovin' with Grit and Grace*, Ronne poignantly writes about her personal experience with remarriage after loss and shares biblical wisdom along with practical tips that leave readers with a roadmap to keep your marriage strong through life's unexpected storms. Ronne even throws in some delicious recipes for good measure, and her husband, Ryan, provides insightful additions as well. Married people at any stage of their relationship will benefit greatly from this book."

—**Ashley Willis,** author of *Peace Pirates*

"This book has the perfect title. With entertaining story telling from her own marriage, Jessica shows the hard work of marriage takes grit but then points the reader toward the grace it takes for a marriage to thrive. I loved how Jessica can write a chapter about diapers and drudgery and take the reader straight to the cross."

—**April Graney,** author of *The Marvelous Mud House*

"What a wonderful addition to the Grit and Grace series! Not only did I find value in the content and thought provoking questions sprinkled throughout the book, but I greatly appreciate the honest perspectives of both Jess and her husband Ryan when tackling the challenging topics that can greatly impact a marriage. Jess has a gift for writing and storytelling that is relatable—I was feeling the humor, frustration, and love with every word."

—**Laurie Hellmann,** author of *Welcome to My Life: A Personal Parenting Journey through Autism*, and host of *Living the Sky Life* podcast

"In *Lovin' with Grit and Grace*, Jess boldly and beautifully talks about the tough, fun, and delicate stuff that makes the journey of marriage adventurous. She invites us into her world while reminding us of how intimately wonderful marriage truly is and that with God's grace, we can experience it in a new and fresh way."

—**Rachel G. Scott,** writer, speaker, Host of *Taking the Leap* Podcast

"I felt so seen in the first few pages, tears started falling. So much of this book accurately described the life my husband and I had been living for fifteen years after severe trauma shattered our lives and left us clinging to one another in an ocean of despair, loneliness, and struggle; all the while wondering if God had abandoned us. If you've ever felt the same, this book will show you spiritual, emotional, and practical steps to learn how to rise above the waves together and find peace, healing, and joy in God and one another . . . no matter what circumstances you are facing."

—**Lindsey Hartz,** author and speaker, and CEO and Lead Marketing Strategist, Hartz Agency / Ignite Faith Media

"Finally, a marriage book that meets most people where they live. Jess and Ryan Ronne live in the trenches where most couples also do, struggling to do the right things in a life that's messy with kids, careers, and all the obstacles to marriage."

—**Brenda L. Yoder,** LMHC, licensed mental health counselor, educator, and author of *Fledge: Launching Your Kids without Losing Your Mind*

"Jess and Ryan openly share about how having a healthy marriage takes grit and a lot of grace to work together through the daily struggles, demands of special needs, a large family, and secrets from their past. It is incredibly encouraging to see them offer hope and practical ways to impact the health and rhythms of your marriage!"

—**Misty Phillip,** Founder of Spark Media, award-winning author, host of *By His Grace* podcast, and cohost of *Spark Influence*

"Marriage can be wonderful and hard at the same time. Jess Ronne's new book, *Lovin' with Grit and Grace*, is filled with deeply personal and relatable stories of the mistakes, love, and heartache of marriage. She tackles the love and sacrifice necessary to a successful relationship with the added stress of blending two families. Let her words invite you into her journey. You'll appreciate her wise and biblical counsel knowing she's been where you are and understands what you're going through."

—**Kate Battistelli,** author of *The God Dare* and *Growing Great Kids*

"Jessica Ronne points your marriage toward connection and deeper intimacy with your spouse in *Lovin' with Grit and Grace*. She addresses the real issues and questions that spouses face with genuine care, humor, and biblical insight. You will be encouraged with every chapter and will find yourself reflecting on every part of your marriage through the lens Jessica so practically and generously shares with us. If you want to grow in your marriage, this book is for you!"

—**Vanessa Martindale,** Founder of Blended Kingdom Families, author of *Blended & Redeemed*

"This book you're holding is a priceless, years-in-the-making gem by Jessica Ronne. The truths within didn't magically emerge from her family life; they were developed over time, intensified by raw and extremely harsh circumstances. The making of a pearl is like the making of a unique, beautiful family. Not one is the same in shape, size, color, or experience. The process includes great aggravation, endurance, yet over time, the grain softens and is shaped into something to be treasured. You will not find another work as authentic and unique; providing wisdom as God shapes your family life into something beautiful."

—**Colleen Swindoll-Thompson,** Founder of Reframing Ministries, Insight for Living

"*Just keep livin'.* Jessica Ronne's signature send-off perhaps rings more clearly in this book than any of the wisdom and insight she has shared about the journey of a caregiver when there is no end to the road of caregiving. *Lovin' with Grit and Grace* is an invitation to vulnerability, honesty, and hope for couples who long for a marriage that is more than wedding rings and well-rehearsed vows. She holds nothing back in this intimate look at everything from sleep and secrets to sex and solitude. The book's conversational style is both practical and hopeful, and Jess and her husband Ryan are unafraid to address topics like the importance of long-road faith and the pain of abuse and pornography. And Jess invites us to the table with recipes that have sustained her family, her marriage, and her own soul for years. *Lovin' with Grit and Grace* should be required reading for all couples longing to 'just keep livin'' a real and abiding relationship."

—**Ronne Rock,** author of *One Woman Can Change the World*

"'Marriage is hard,' said everyone who's been married longer than ten minutes. Jess and Ryan show us how to endure through the hard parts while intentionally finding joy in the everyday moments. With endearing stories woven into a memorable acronym (HISHERS), this book will show you God's heart for today's marriage."

— **Amy Lively,** author of *How to Love Your Neighbor Without Being Weird* and *Hope Fully*

"Jess Ronne and her hubby deliver a fantastic book to help us all keep our marriages spicy, fun, and devoted to one another. *Lovin' with Grit and Grace*—written in Ronne's signature style of real, witty, and practical—is a must-read. I came away encouraged and ready to implement her tips in my own relationship. I devoured this book. Reading it was like being on a double-date full of heart to hearts, good wine, and outbursts of giggling."

— **Sarah Philpott,** author of *The Growing Season: A Year of Down on the Farm Devotions* and *Loved Baby: 31 Devotions Helping You Grieve and Cherish Your Baby after Pregnancy Loss*

LOVIN'
WITH
GRIT & GRACE

To my husband Ryan, grow old with me,
the best is yet to be.

To my children, may his favor be upon you for a
thousand generations and your family and your
children and their children and their children.

To my faithful Savior and Lord,
thank you for the gift of life.

Just keep livin'!

LOVIN'
WITH
GRIT & GRACE

STRAIGHT TALK ABOUT ROMANCE,
SEX, FUN, AND THE TOUGH STUFF TOO

Jessica Ronne

LEAFWOOD
PUBLISHERS
an imprint of Abilene Christian University Press

LOVIN' WITH GRIT AND GRACE

Straight Talk about Romance, Sex, Fun, and the Tough Stuff Too

LEAFWOOD
P U B L I S H E R S
an imprint of Abilene Christian University Press

Copyright © 2023 by Jessica Ronne

ISBN 978-68426-092-8

Printed in the United States of America

Published in association with Stephanie Alton of The Blythe Daniel Agency, Inc., PO Box 64197, Colorado Springs, CO 80962.

Cataloging-in-Publication Data is on file at the Library of Congress, Washington, DC.

Cover design by Thinkpen Design, LLP
Interior text design by Strong Design, Sandy Armstrong

Leafwood Publishers is an imprint of Abilene Christian University Press
ACU Box 29138
Abilene, Texas 79699

1-877-816-4455
www.leafwoodpublishers.com

23 24 25 26 27 28 29 / 8 7 6 5 4 3 2

CONTENTS

> Consistency Is Key
> Walking through the Seasons of Life
> Winter Walk
> In Sickness and in Health
> Psalm 23 and Self-Care
> Health and the Caregiver
> Bedtime
> Pruning for Self-Care

> Words That Wound
> See Me
> See Me Too
> Finding Your Voice
> Releasing Control
> Spring Walks—Dealing with Your Anger
> Vulnerable Moments
> Ignorance Is Not Bliss
> Sharing Your Fears
> Don't Look in the Rearview Mirror
> Restoration

> Desire Starts with You
> Desire Me Too
> Sexual Graveyards
> The Day Everything Changed
> Snapshots
> Obstacles to Sex
> Spice Is Nice
> Boundaries
> Bargains and Schedules

FOREWORD

Discovering "Jess Plus the Mess" on Facebook in 2012 was like finding a unicorn. I didn't know any other couples who took a flying leap of faith into a new life after losing their first spouses to cancer. Like Ryan and Jess, my husband Michael and I blended our families, started a nonprofit, wrote a book (that became a Hallmark movie), and live a messy, unpredictable, and chaotic life built on the hope we have in Jesus.

Experiencing Jess through her writing is to experience 2 Corinthians 1:3–5: "Praise be to the God and Father of our Lord Jesus Christ, the Father of compassion and the God of all comfort, who comforts us in all our troubles, so that we can comfort those in any trouble with the comfort we ourselves received from God. For just as we share abundantly in the sufferings of Christ, so also our comfort abounds through Christ." I was understood, validated, and not alone in my circumstances.

Jess is a vulnerable, honest, and authentic writer, and person. She handles sensitive subject matter with the kind of delicate honesty that elicits responses ranging from fist pumping to laughing out loud to flat out feeling convicted. Her words stir the soul as they expose the heart-wrenching underbelly of marriage with the kind of vulnerability and transparency that make you feel known. This gift offers us the strength to persevere.

Jess has used her experience and wisdom to become a beacon of hope for a stressed-out, worked-up, freaked-out world. She is credentialed, and her voice rises above the noise of the "do more, be more, pursue more" world, reminding us we can choose to move forward with faith and tend to all our "special needs" . . . not only special needs children, but also the special needs we have as individuals to care for ourselves.

Throughout the book Jess seamlessly sprinkles in recipes for delicious and comforting foods. The recipes flow in and out of chapters like the day-to-day process of feeding a family, as if while writing she looked up and realized, *I have eight hungry mouths to feed!*

But the real recipes are those baked in, sautéed, and simmering throughout the book, using "Health, Intimacy, Sex, Household tasks, Excitement, Romance, and Spirituality" as the key ingredients. This isn't a sugary, processed dish that lacks substance. No, this is real sustenance and nourishment for husbands, wives, and marriages that will help us go the distance while under the watchful eyes and listening ears of our children.

Whether newlywed or celebrating a golden anniversary, the tenderness, simplicity, and raw truth on these pages will give you the strength to persevere and live with hope. I'm thankful to Jess and Ryan for their courage in writing this book and for the privilege of reading the intimate details of their life. Their words are a reminder to walk closely with God to be continually refined and reshaped for his purposes in your marriage.

Gina Spehn
Author of *Color of Rain* (turned into a Hallmark movie)
Cofounder and President of New Day Foundation for Families

INTRODUCTION

The words we need to say are usually paired with a look that says *I mean business*, and it almost always requires immediate attention. We've all witnessed a scene in a movie where this scenario is portrayed, and the entire set goes quiet and heartbreak follows. Have you noticed this too? "We need to talk" is often followed by a call for change and a whole lot of tears. I'm guessing you are thinking of the last time you heard or even said this phrase and realized something was about to pivot in your life. Maybe it was a sudden change that crushed your heart.

It was those four simple words that paved the way for a big change in my marriage; including the ideas for growth that followed. Let me set the scene for you.

"We need to talk." I gave my husband Ryan a look that indicated there was a deep conversation looming on the horizon.

He quickly shimmied his way to the couch and rested his feet upon the coffee table. February was usually when we vacationed in Mexico, but this year we opted out of warm sunny skies and ocean breezes and opted in to a weeklong "vacation" at a local Airbnb where we spent our days clearing trees from our recently purchased parcel of land in Michigan that we were preparing for a future build. Mexico, Michigan—the exact same, right?!

After seven years in Tennessee, we made the difficult decision to move back to my hometown where we hoped to receive the support and resources needed for our large family and for our disabled son Lucas. We were leaving a state we had called home for seven years, a place where we often found ourselves panicky and frantic and clinging to one another for dear life; we were drowning in an ocean of responsibility, one of us going beneath the surface while the other was coming up for air, oftentimes pushed back down by the weight of the never-ending tasks with no life preservers in sight. No one to help. And now we were building a new dream in Michigan, a life built on the premise of community—friends and family who knew us and would throw us a life preserver if needed.

And now, here we sat, suspiciously looking at one another, inhaling a delicious pizza after an exhausting day of cutting down trees and moving logs, but I wasn't content. No, in fact I could feel the stream of tears starting to rise out of frustration.

"What's wrong?" he cautiously questioned.

"Well," I hesitantly continued, "we've been on vacation for a few days, and I've been harping for months about the lack of romance in our relationship. You've continued to assure me for *months* that 'it'll change as soon as we go on vacation,' because you have a hard time being romantic with the stresses of daily life and eight kids and special needs and work. And actually, you promised 'all the romance I can handle on vacation,' and I've given you grace. I've held out hope for this magical promise of a romantic vacation.

I've eagerly anticipated our time together and worked my tail end off, hauling logs as a forty-three-year-old middle-aged woman— trying to make you proud. Trying to entice you to do something super romantic and nothing has changed. You're still exhausted and stressed, and I'm still disappointed."

I blurted out my passionate plea and slumped back into the couch, eager to shove another piece of pizza into my starving, weary, and unromanced body. I expected an immediate apology or at the very least an excuse, but instead I received spitfire anger. My husband was ticked off.

"I've been working for months," he began, "never taking a break, going far above and beyond what my body is probably even capable of—especially after a shoulder surgery only a year ago!—and you're complaining about romance? Seriously? I'm *always* romantic! I help with the dishes every day. We walk together. We pray together in the morning! We have a consistent sex life; and you think I'm not romantic?! Really? Most women would kill for what you get!"

Now I was disgusted, frustrated, and mad.

"You think sex and praying are romance? Seriously? You don't understand women at all!" I shoved the last morsel of pizza into my mouth and stormed off to the bathtub to wash the angst out of my soul.

I allowed the warm water and soothing lavender bubbles to calm my racing heart, and Ryan used the silence that followed our heated argument to reflect. I emerged thirty minutes later with a slower heart rate and was ready to ignore my husband for the remainder of the night; however, while I had been stewing in the bath, he had been thinking. I hesitantly rejoined him in the family room and slowly met his gaze.

"You know," he said, "you're right. I thought those things— dishes, walks, prayers, and sex—were romance. As men, we're taught that sex begins in the kitchen; and in my mind, if I'm doing the dishes, I'm romancing you for later that night."

I sat there dumbstruck. My husband seriously thought doing the dishes was romantic? Oh boy. It was going to be a long night.

"Explain it to me," he continued. "I want to know! I need to understand."

And that began our exploration into the question of what romance looks like in a relationship. How is its perception different for men and women? What does romance look like for me personally? We stayed up late that night questioning, laughing, and exploring these concepts, which eventually led to a fun little acronym that has been extremely helpful in our journey toward understanding the differences and expectations we each bring to our relationship. The acronym is simply His & Hers. Seven letters (most of you know how much I love my sevens): HISHERS—which stand for seven important categories in a marriage.

H—Health

I—Intimacy

S—Sex

H—Household

E—Excitement

R—Romance

S—Spirituality

All seven categories are imperative for a healthy, robust, and growing marriage, but some have more importance to one partner than the other. Each category should receive consistent check-ups for the relationship to maintain respect and growth. The unique nature of His & Hers is that some couples will require more checks in certain categories than others. Some women might want a lot of checks in the sex box, while others may not. Some men might require more checks in the intimacy box and not require as many checks in the sex box. Some women might need a lot of new activities and excitement—tango classes, yes! Cooking club, yes! Movie night, yes! And some may rather have the dishes done every single day.

It's about moving intentionally, step by step, and communicating about which categories are most important to you as an individual and to your marriage, and then setting realistic goals to attain what's needed in these areas. For example, I want more romance, yes, yes, yes! Romance to me is *not* doing the dishes or praying together. Doing the dishes falls under the household category and praying falls under the spiritual category. Romance for me is a candlelit dinner, flowers, or little notes of endearment left on a steamy mirror. In a perfect world, I'd appreciate some semblance of romance once a month. Laundry, dishes, and clean floors are not that big of a deal, but romance is. Another woman reading this might think I'm crazy and may want clean dishes every day, and perhaps that is romance for her! That's where effective communication factors in as you help your partner understand your needs and expectations.

Admittedly, marriage is never easy. Never, ever, ever. Fulfilling? Absolutely. Growth inducing? Positively. Worth it? Yes, in my opinion. We are now eleven years into marriage together after our first spouses passed away in 2010; eleven years with seven then eight children, special needs, autism, lingering grief, and adoption. Statistically speaking, 67 percent of second marriages and 23 percent of marriages with an autism diagnosis end in divorce.[1] I think that gives my marriage about a 10 percent chance of making it; but here we are, still standing. No, it's not perfect, but what Ryan and I have is pretty darn special and worth celebrating. Our relationship has blossomed from two naive thirty-four-year-olds secretly running off to the courthouse to get married (Yep! More on that admission later) into a respectful and loving union through reliance on the Lord, communication, and, let's face it, effort. Good old fashioned elbow grease, which includes checking in with one another and occasionally peeling back the perception of peace to expose the real issues that might be lurking beneath the surface. And believe me, every relationship has those issues!

What works for us may not work for everyone, and this is where these categories provide boundaries for communication to occur so lasting change can take effect. The key to these seven categories is consistency, and this includes an occasional check-in about what is important individually and collectively. Most couples yearn for change but simply don't know how to bring it to the table. It's difficult to admit that there might be something lacking in a relationship or to rock the boat when things seem to be somewhat peaceful; however, that peace is often a façade if we're not addressing issues, and that façade has the potential of exploding into a much bigger issue if we don't face our resentments.

That's where I hope and pray *Lovin' with Grit and Grace* can provide a gentle road map for any marital relationship that seeks clarification, simplification, or maybe a firm kick in the rear end. Maybe you and your spouse need hope, or a walk together, or simply a good recipe—which are occasionally shared because "the way to a man's heart" and all that jazz. Sound good? Alrighty, find a comfy chair, put up your feet, and let's dive into the ways these categories have played out in our marriage and how you might find similar success through incorporating these seven principles.

Just keep livin'!

Jess

NOTE

[1] Mark Banschick, "The High Failure Rate of Second and Third Marriages," *Psychology Today*, February 6, 2012, https://www.psychologytoday.com/us/blog/the-intelligent-divorce/201202/the-high-failure-rate-second-and-third-marriages; Stephen Grcevich, "Special Needs and Divorce: What Does the Data Say?," Key Ministry, March 28, 2016, https://www.keyministry.org/church4everychild/2016/3/28/special-needs-and-divorce-what-does-the-data-say?rq=divorce%20rate.

1

HEALTH

Preserving This Commodity in Our Marriages

"Jess, they want to schedule a PET scan. They think it might be cancer."

I heard these words from Ryan in 2017, and they rocked my world. We were living what we thought was our dream life in rural Tennessee: raising our children, tilling the land, butchering chickens, and renovating houses. Only a few years earlier, we had left everything we had ever known to pursue the simple life, and now Ryan was facing numerous health scares, including the discovery of spots on his lungs, a thirty-pound weight loss, and trips to the emergency room. I wanted to scream, "Are you out of your mind, Lord?! You took one husband and left me as a widow with four kids. Are you seriously going to do this again? Cancer with eight children? In the middle of nowhere?!"

And I began to panic. I set systems in place to make my family even healthier than we already were. Intense systems created out of fear, like no sugar or carbs; only organic, free-range meats and vegetables; lots of elixirs and cancer-killing teas; and energy workout videos on YouTube. I needed something to occupy my thoughts, and instead of turning to prayer, I turned to control.

Now, we do have a role to play in our health and should strive to do the best we can. This is a biblical principle—"Do you not know that your bodies are temples of the Holy Spirit, who is in you, whom you have received from God? You are not your own" (1 Cor. 6:19)—but there is also a time and a place to surrender and give it to the Lord: "Come to me, all who labor and are heavy laden, and I will give you rest" (Matt. 11:28 ESV).

Ryan and I have had many encounters with death and scary diagnoses, which have led to our marital efforts to maintain a healthy lifestyle; although it has not been the easiest endeavor while caring for a disabled child. The experts state that 53 percent of caregivers claim that caring for a loved one has worsened their health, which was part of Ryan's problems.[1] He is a "put your head down and get 'er done" kind of guy; and instead of acknowledging and releasing the stress in his body, Ryan allowed the stress to build and fester, which led to numerous trips to the ER, weight loss, and the conversation where he said, "Jess they want to schedule a PET scan. They think it might be cancer."

Cancer. The most feared word in most people's vocabulary, including mine. A word that experts claim is avoidable by 80 percent of people who get it.[2] Since we do have some control over the process, I'm going to do my part to maintain a joyful, healthy life with my family for as long as the Lord grants me breath in my lungs. Our health is a gift and should be consistently prioritized— all aspects of our health, including our diets and our mental health.

We should care about this precious commodity not only for ourselves but also for those we love.

Consistency Is Key

Throughout our eleven years together, Ryan and I have diligently incorporated daily and weekly routines to prioritize healthy habits; and yes, these habits have arrived through consistently choosing what may not be the most pleasurable option in order to reap the long-term benefits. You know what I'm talking about. Making a fresh salad instead of running through the McDonalds drive-through on the way home from work. Or setting the alarm to get a morning run in because you know you won't do it at the end of the day. Or putting your phone away and reading a book instead of obsessing about what the neighbors are doing. These are choices we make to reap the long-term benefits of health, and this consistency is the cornerstone to our success with busy lives.

I'm pretty sure I come by these traits honestly. I grew up with parents who each made daily to-do lists. I'm also the granddaughter of Sarella and Leonard Bossebroek. Leonard was a respected pastor and Sally, his wife, was a nurse turned homemaker after giving birth to their four sons. I vividly remember as a young girl visiting my grandparent's home and being told to *not bother Grandpa in the basement* because he was preparing for his Sunday sermon. Sometimes I would tiptoe down the steps when Grandma was busy and peek around the corner to find Grandpa hunched over his desk, glasses perched high upon his face, pouring over the Bible and other commentaries that would help him formulate the sermon he would preach on Sunday. He would stay in this posture for hours, diligently studying and praying for wisdom until Grandma would call down, "Dad! It's time for your afternoon walk!" and up the stairs he sauntered, put on his spirit walking shoes (with galoshes if weather called for them) and a lightweight

Polo jacket, and ventured off for his daily walk. I'm not entirely sure how long his walks were, but he prioritized them almost every day. Grandpa was also diagnosed with type 2 diabetes in his older age, and Grandma made sure to use this diagnosis to reprimand him whenever he tried to add an extra spoonful of sugar to his morning corn flakes—the same daily breakfast he'd eaten for years. He'd wink at me as he tried to sneak this spoonful of sugar only to have Grandma whip her head around from the kitchen and declare, "Dad! You know you can't have that with your diabetes." "Oh right, Mom," he'd mutter, slowly putting the spoon back into the sugar container. But it wasn't only that Grandma took care of Grandpa. If she looked worn out or tired, he was quick to suggest that she lie down for a bit. And often she would oblige, although I'm not sure she slept much. They took care of each other and, as "iron sharpens iron," looked out for one another's best interests when it came to their health. The key to their longevity (they both lived to be in their nineties!) was consistency with many of these small daily practices.

Consistency is a theme that will pop up time and time again throughout our stories. This isn't an exciting word or a sexy concept, but it is the glue to a healthy, happy relationship and a healthy, happy life! The word "consistency" is cousins with words like "rhythms" and "routines," and these ebbs and flows are what balance us and bring us back into communion with our Maker and with one another. These routines also instruct us in what it means to be a human being. Since the beginning of time, humanity has had its roots in rhythms. In Genesis we read that the Lord created the world in six days and rested on the seventh. He made the sun, moon, and stars to dictate the circadian rhythms so that we would know when to sleep and when to rise. Everything in creation follows a pattern for survival—the rising and the setting of the sun, the lunar cycles, the months, the seasons, and the years steadily marching forward—so it makes sense that our bodies operate optimally within cycles and seasons as well. Individually, this looks like rising with the sun and sleeping with the moon, or working six days a week as our Lord modeled and resting on the Sabbath, or gathering our harvest in the summer and relaxing in the cooler winter months. When our body is in rhythm with nature, we give ourselves an optimal chance at maintaining optimal health.

Ryan and I prioritize a handful of rhythms that help maintain the seven categories we are going to address: health, intimacy, sex, household, excitement, romance, and spirituality. We pray together, walk together, drink tea together, and garden together (weather permitting). We cook together, making homemade pasta or brick oven pizzas on the patio. We head to bed and watch our shows and turn off the lights together. We have many dynamics and busy schedules, so most of our routines occur at home, but perhaps it's different for your family. Maybe you like to get out of the house and participate in triathlons or enjoy family days at the gym.

Whatever this looks like for your situation, remember, these are the intimate moments that build a life together. These are the moments we will look back on fondly at the end of our days and recall—the good stuff, the stuff we dwell on as the angels escort us to glory. Some of these are seasonal rhythms, some annual, and others daily. They provide structure for our busy lives and a framework to slow down and breathe—a framework individually and for our relationships. These routines speak life into our weariness as we set aside our personal agendas to enjoy these joint priorities with a partner we love. They also provide a loose framework for maintaining health and vitality in our busy schedules as we habitually return to the basis of our beliefs, which is really what these rhythms and routines consist of.

Health is so much more than the foods we choose to put in our bodies; it's a state of mind and includes our daily choices. Choices to exercise and go to bed on time. Choices to face any addictions that may hinder our relationships. Choices to pursue self-care and rest so we don't end up in the hospital. And nine times out of ten, these choices will lead to a life of health and vitality or a life of prescription drugs and pain.

What consistent choices are you making as a family? Where might you need to improve? Think through these questions with your spouse and then commit to making one small change this week. You'll thank yourself for it in the long run.

Quick and Easy Salad

I often have most of these ingredients on hand to make this quick and easy salad instead of running through a drive-through somewhere. And yes, I top it with homemade ranch because I deserve a reward for all the vegetables.

- Bag of mixed greens
- Red onion
- Bacon bits
- Grilled chicken
- Avocado
- Cherry tomatoes
- Optional, fresh mozzarella cut into small pieces
- Ranch dressing seasoning packet

Mix the ingredients together to make the homemade ranch and chill for about an hour. Next, toss the remaining ingredients together and enjoy!

Walking through the Seasons of Life

"Honey! Are you ready to walk?" I hollered to Ryan who was sitting in our office catching up on some paperwork. "Yep! Just give me a minute," he quickly replied.

Walking is an activity we enjoy and has been a part of my health routine for as long as I can remember. When I was a teenager, my mom and I would relieve the monotonous boredom of homeschooled life by walking up and down our dusty road together. I shared tidbits of my soul, and she would share about her life. I enjoyed the calming nature walking lent to my overthinking ways, and continued this habit into my college years. I often met friends at the local track or snuck off alone on the weekends to a hiking trail to gather my thoughts about life, faith, and men.

After my marriage to Jason, I continued to walk. Sometimes I would hurry home after work to rip off my teaching clothes and replace them with comfy sweatpants and a T-shirt before heading off to Kent Trails—a long winding stretch of paths only minutes from our apartment. Sometimes Jason would tag along; but more often than not, he was still at work, and walking wasn't his idea of fitness. He was a tennis professional and personal trainer, so he opted for heavy lifting and left the walking to his wife.

Now, at forty-four years old, I've walked through many seasons of life. I've fought through bitter cold winters in Michigan that require long johns beneath sweatpants and down coats, topped off with hats, mittens, and scarves. I've walked in the blazing southern sun as it stretched high in the sky, scorching my brow and anything else I dared to lay bare beneath her fiery rays, kicking up dusty red dirt as I shuffled along. I've walked with a brace on my leg after breaking my foot, and only days after losing my baby to a miscarriage—breathing deeply with each step as I chose to move toward life. I walked down to the Tennessee River in our backyard to pray after having my baby girl, and in doing so regained strength in both body and soul after almost losing my life during her tumultuous birth. I've walked beside husbands and friends and children and babies. I've pushed strollers and double strollers! I've trudged through rain, sunshine, sleet, and snow. I've worn sunglasses for most of my walks to hide the tears when they unexpectedly arrive—which they do more often than not as I pray for those who are hurting and sometimes those prayers are turned on myself. My walks remind me that this is how this life gig works. Step by step. Moment by moment. Walking is therapeutic and reflective and where clarity is revealed, often through the same songs I've listened to year after year. Songs of encouragement for my weary heart. Songs like Natalie Grant's "I will Not Be Moved" and Francesca Battistelli's "Beautiful, Beautiful" or Kelly Clarkson's "What Doesn't Kill You Makes You Stronger." I never tire of these songs because they're a part of me and a part of my rhythm. I allow the words to penetrate my heart during seasons when the sun shines upon me, each step full of life and vigor, or when the sun doesn't shine and I find myself in a season of pushing against the bitter cold, and I dare her outstretched arms to stop my movement forward; literally willing each step as a prayer toward deliverance as I plead for healing from whatever demons torment me.

Ryan often accompanies me on these walks as we've found that the couple who walks together, talks together, and maybe loses a pound or two. Walking has helped as we've wrestled with issues of abandonment, betrayal, blendedness, and special needs. Our life can be heavy at times, but as we've learned with our walking routine, we choose to move forward, step by step, trusting that the Lord's faithfulness will sustain and provide us with what we need for the moment, even if we find ourselves walking in the midst of a bitter cold night as I once did in December of 2009.

Winter Walk

Life can be hard, and we often find ourselves in a period that doesn't make any sense. A period of betrayal or abandonment, or a child who seems to be headed down a dangerous path—circumstances we would wish away in an instant if we could. I found myself in one such period in December of 2009. My late husband Jason was battling brain cancer, and it was becoming increasingly difficult for him to engage in life because of the treatments and the effects they had on his energy and mental health. I often walked through the snow on these dark nights as I willed myself to feel alive; to feel the bite against my face and keep moving in spite of how weary I had become.

On one of these particular evenings, the children lay nestled in their warm beds, oblivious to the torment I felt, and as Jason reclined pale and motionless in his reclining chair, I wrapped myself in a thick coat, pulled boots upon my weary feet, and ventured out into the bitter loneliness. My emergence was greeted by a silent dirt road, my being enveloped by the brisk air as the blackness provided shelter from the rest of humanity. Nothing but stillness awaited my pilgrimage. I felt free.

I glanced to the left and recognized a spattering of houses and to the right, nothing but naked branches swayed in the stagnant air. I leaned into the vacancy and began to move, one foot in front of the other, the vicious cold nipping my face and freezing the tears as they fell. I walked in penance for whatever grave sin I had committed—a sin which had led to a life of pain and heartache. I knew that surely if my husband had the strength to wage war against numerous rounds of poison, and my son had the strength to defy the proclamations of death voiced against him, and my children possessed the strength to look into the abyss of eternity staring back at them through their daddy's hollow gaze, then surely—*surely*—I could face whatever lay ahead. And so, I walked.

I walked the coals, the clear crystal coals intermingled with the frozen ground. And nothing moved. And all was silent.

I walked, and I paused, and I crumpled to the earth, fists curled and pumping into the night sky. "*Curse you night!*" I screamed.

I screamed until the noise was deafened by gasps, gasps of oxygen being pumped into a broken heart, gasps of air reviving a weary soul, and then I rose, yet again, to face my tormentor and fell beneath the weight of the heavy cold air. I wrestled and rose and cursed and moaned again and again to the beat of the maestro's baton, to the beat of the never-ending drum of life.

Eventually I grew weary, as we all do, and I turned back, slowly fixing my gaze to reality, the dim lights flickering through the swaying trees, ready to return to my life—a haven of pain and grief and joy.

I still walk in the bitter air, but I no longer seek the solitude of the night. I now turn to face the warmth of the sun, often walking hand in hand with those I love—those born of the light, like my baby girl Annabelle. I've walked through the bitter cold of what was and the warmth of what is, learning how life can unravel at any moment into something bright and beautiful and unexpected.

I am choosing life, choosing warmth, and choosing to keep moving forward, as we all must do.

In Sickness and in Health

In March of 2011, after I had accepted Ryan's proposal, I ventured to his hometown in Oklahoma to pack for our move to Michigan. I had been going nonstop for years. Jason died in August of 2010, and that's when I became a single mom of four young children—an exhausting endeavor. And then I met Ryan, and we had a whirlwind courtship as we traveled back and forth to visit, often meeting halfway and sometimes bringing the children and mourning the deaths of our first spouses while simultaneously grieving our time apart. It was way too much.

As we loaded the U-Haul truck with Ryan's belongings, I realized how exhausted I was. My eyes burned and my back ached and my whole body was bone weary tired, but I chalked it up to how busy we had been over the past couple of months. I figured I could sleep all the way to Kansas, which was the midway point to Michigan and where we would rest for the night. I climbed in beside my fiancé and waved goodbye to the only life Ryan had ever known, waved goodbye to his friends and family, and waved goodbye to his home. I shimmied a pillow up against the window and laid my head against the rattling door.

"Tired babe?" Ryan asked loudly, trying to be heard against the backdrop of the exhaust system.

"Yeah," I responded wearily. "I'm going to rest my eyes for a bit. Wake me up if you need anything."

That was the last thing I said before I heard Ryan whispering, "Jess, Jess. We made it to Kansas. You slept the whole way." I slowly lifted my head and glanced out at the night sky. Sure enough, we weren't in Oklahoma anymore. The flickering lights from the cheap hotel's neon sign stared back at me.

"Gosh, I don't know why I'm so tired," I lamented as we checked in for the night. I dove onto my bed and slept deeply but awoke the next morning still feeling exhausted. We continued our exodus toward Michigan and arrived around dusk. We unloaded the truck and said hello to my kids. Ryan's kids had stayed behind with grandparents who promised to transport them to Michigan after we were settled. I paid the babysitter and then headed home to sleep. Ryan had purchased a home in Michigan, but I continued to live at my house until we were married because it seemed like the right thing to do. Once home, I climbed into bed and zonked out again. Around midnight I awoke, drenched in sweat and shaking uncontrollably. I didn't want to wake Ryan who had just had an exhausting day of travel—especially since I had been so out of commission. I took a few Advil, attributed my malaise to the flu, and tried to go back to sleep. I continued to wake up every hour, drenched in sweat and hallucinating about the characters of Sesame Street, in my room, playing duck, duck, goose. Their insistence that I play this game while I attempted to sleep really annoyed me.

When morning arrived, my whole body ached. I somehow managed to get Caleb and Lucas off to school, and then I called Ryan.

I choked out the words, "Honey, I don't feel good. I think I might need to go to an Urgent Care."

"Really?" he responded. "That bad?"

"I can't stop shaking," I replied, my teeth chattering, "and my back is killing me."

"Okay, I'll be right over," he promised.

While I waited, I contacted the babysitter, and she agreed to watch Mabel and Josh.

Ryan took one glance at me, pale, shaking, and holding my back in agony, and told me to get in the van. He rushed me to the ER, where a few tests later we learned I had a really bad kidney infection, and I was going to be admitted. It was the worst news on so many levels. First, I hate pain, and I hate needles even more. I pretty much cried throughout my entire stay. Second, talk about anxiety for Ryan and his kids. Here I was supposed to be his healthy fiancée, about to be his wife after the sudden death of his first wife, and then I get really sick and end up in ER for a few days! And this is what Ryan's children arrived in Michigan to discover: their soon-to-be new mom in the hospital. Talk about traumatic.

I was admitted, administered a strong dose of antibiotics, and discharged three days later—still exhausted but feeling a little bit more myself. That was a hard lesson to learn. I had been immersed in a life of consistently going too hard for too long; whereas, if I had incorporated small and consistent acts of self-care, slowed down, not talked to Ryan until midnight every day, and pursued the sleep and hydration my body required, I probably could have curtailed the entire experience all together. I vowed to do better in the future. Better for myself and better for my family who depended on me and was about to grow quite expansive!

Psalm 23 and Self-Care

As a busy working mom, I find it's terribly easy to *do*. *Do* more, *be* more, pursue more, and it's this doing and not enough resting that landed my rear end in an ER room with a kidney infection only months before my wedding day.

It's easy for me to accomplish because doing and being and pursuing and striving are celebrated in our culture. It's noble to pile all the things on our weary shoulders: climb higher, reach for the stars, never, ever quit or give up. It's much more difficult to stop. To rest. To not do. To lie down in green pastures and pursue silence as King David writes about in Psalm 23, where he sets aside his work and pursues peace, stillness, and rest.

When I first received confirmation from my publisher that, yes, they wanted this book, they asked if I could I have it finished by October 2021. I know myself. I could have risen to the challenge because I am not the best at resting and often operate from a "get 'er done" mindset. At first, I responded, "Sure! No problem!" But then I paused. Was this really the best idea? To push this hard in the middle of a move from Tennessee to Michigan? In the middle of building a house? And restructuring a nonprofit? And hosting a podcast? And planning a graduation party for my two oldest? And a being filmed with my family for a documentary project? Oh yeah, and raising a bushel full of children?

I knew I could have a book finished by October 2021 if I had to; but at what cost, I wondered. So I prayed about it. I brought the dilemma to my faithful shepherd, and he said, *ask for an extension*. How do I know he said this? Because I did not feel a peace about having the book finished by October, and when I asked for an extension, my publisher granted the request immediately. Now I'm not maxed out beyond my human capabilities, and this book will still get written (as evidenced by your holding it now!). The Lord met me where I was and provided a solution.

I love learning from the example of King David's life. If anyone understood the concept of fight or flight—a concept I understand well in my busy life—it would have been David as he appeared to live his life mostly in this frantic mode of operation. However, upon a closer glance at his story, which does include fighting and running and making bad decisions that often led to consequences, we also find a man who was well-versed in self-care.

David journaled his feelings, as we witness throughout Psalms. He sang songs of worship to the Lord. He made love to his wife. He gathered in community and feasted and danced! He rested in green pastures. He prayed. He enjoyed the beauty of nature and allowed his soul to find rest in the presence of music.

We can learn a lot about the different forms of self-care by studying the life of David and specifically Psalm 23 (NKJV), which I often use as a prayer when life begins to feel out of control.

The LORD is my shepherd; I shall not want.

I release my cares, worries, and desire to control the situation. I give it to you Lord and trust your sovereign will over my life.

He makes me to lie down in green pastures;

Part of self-care might involve me laying down my will for productivity and embracing your will for rest. Part of this rest may involve literally lying down in the beautiful gift of nature you've provided, or maybe it's lying down in my bed and taking a nap instead of pursuing more productivity.

He leads me beside the still waters.

Self-care might look like taking a stroll in nature and breathing in the fresh air you have blessed me with. It might include putting aside the spreadsheet and instead spending time with my husband or children at a park.

He restores my soul; He leads me in the paths of righteousness for His name's sake.

Oh Lord, restore my weary soul. Breathe peace and wisdom into all the spaces of confusion and overwhelm. Lead me into your paths of righteousness and then give me the strength to obey whatever calling you have placed upon my life.

Yea, though I walk through the valley of the
shadow of death, I will fear no evil; for You are
with me; Your rod and Your staff, they comfort me.

Lord, as I walk through difficult periods of life,
often overflowing with fear or drama or dismay, be
my comfort and my shield. Provide me with a peace
that passes understanding so that I might stand
firm in whatever circumstance life throws my way.

You prepare a table before me in the
presence of my enemies; You anoint my
head with oil; my cup runs over.

As I battle enemies of self-doubt or unworthiness,
may I pause. May I invite a good friend over for
dinner where we feast upon wood-fire pizza and
wine. May the gift of fellowship strengthen me and
propel me forward in this life.

Surely goodness and mercy shall follow
me all the days of my life; and I will dwell
in the house of the LORD forever.

Lord, I choose you. I choose your goodness, which is
not found in constant doing and striving. I choose
to believe your promise for my life, and I choose
everlasting mercy in this life and the next. I choose
to walk beside you all my days until I breathe
my last.

Folks, let's be brave enough to walk away from chaos and the to-do list and the never-ending chores. Let's be brave enough to trust that the Lord will meet us and comfort our weary hearts and bless us with rest and joy and a table overflowing with community. Let's be bold enough to obey and step away to provide a space for self-care to grow in ourselves and in our marriages.

Health and the Caregiver

I awoke in extreme pain in my hips, back, and neck—the same story for years—and I did what I do most mornings. I got Lucas ready for school and then laced up my shoes and embarked on a two-mile walk to loosen my joints and shake off the stress.

And as I walked, I glanced up at the bright blue sky and noticed the beautiful fall colors that resembled a rainbow, and I wept, thankful for sunglasses that hid any vulnerability from the cars whizzing by.

Being Lucas's mom has broken me in a million ways throughout the past seventeen years: mentally, spiritually, emotionally, and most profoundly, physically. My body is in constant pain, and I do most things right. I eat healthy 80 percent of the time. I work out most days. I stretch. I go to the chiropractor. I get acupuncture. I spend 5 million dollars on supplements so I can live forever. I schedule massages. I take vacations. And I'm still always in pain. The specialists tell me to "get my stress under control." But how, I wonder, when I live in a continuous state of fight or flight as I care for a seventeen-year-old with profound needs; my beautiful son who is aging and, in the process, becoming stronger and more opinionated and aggressive at times.

This problem isn't unique to me. The majority of special needs caregivers I've met or talked to throughout the years have mentioned the negative side effects related to being a caregiver. Some are mild, such as headaches, irritable bowel syndrome, or weight fluctuations, and other symptoms are not so mild and can land a caregiver on the road to rehabilitation for months, if not years. This was the story for Vance Goforth, a caregiver I interviewed on my podcast. He had a heart attack due to the stress associated with caring for his son Joshua, who has profound special needs and autism.

Statistically, 43 percent of caregivers for those with special needs admit that being a caregiver contributes to high stress, and 26 percent say their health is fair to poor (compared to 15 percent of the general public).[3]

Ryan and I have experienced numerous side effects from being caregivers—not only for Lucas but for seven other children as well. I don't believe every symptom is directly related to the stress of being a caregiver, but I do believe most of them can be traced back to stress.

A few years ago, it was hair loss, which began when Lucas ended up in the ER in December 2019 due to a shunt malfunction. He finally returned to school in the middle of February but then was released from school indefinitely (along with everyone else) in March 2020. He and his siblings were all released and home for months. This was one of the most difficult times of my life—even more so on many levels than my late husband's three-year battle with cancer. It was around the end of April 2020 that I noticed the large chunks of hair falling out every time I brushed it. Or took a shower. Or simply shook my head. And I freaked out. I seriously thought, *This is it. I'm going bald.*

Of course, I did what anyone would do and immediately headed to Google, which confirmed my worst fears. Yes, high amounts of stress over a prolonged period can cause hair loss, but within six to nine months of the stress being remedied, the hair loss should diminish. I gave myself about six months to complete baldness because I had no idea how I was going to relieve my stress levels during pandemic living.

So, I did the only thing I could do: I started to slowly, step-by-step, put a plan in place that included practicing breath work to mitigate the flight or fight response in which my body typically operated, taking prenatal vitamins, and using expensive hair elixirs. I guzzled bone broth, which is full of collagen! I attacked the problem in true Jessica fashion, which made me feel better but probably didn't help much, as I simply had to be patient and wait. My hair did finally grow back, mostly. It's still pretty thin two years later, but it's not falling out in chunks anymore.

It's good to be proactive by admitting the issue and then trying to change a situation that's gone off the rails. Make that appointment with the doctor or masseuse or invest in some supplements that might help. But in other scenarios, it's simply a waiting game. Our circumstances aren't going to change overnight, but we can take small steps to improve the situation. Overweight? Commit to a daily dance workout on YouTube. Home with a child with special needs? Dance in front of him or her, and call it entertainment for the day—yes, true story with Lucas.

Being a caregiver is hard and holy work, and as caregivers, we must consistently prioritize those tiny drops of self-care throughout our days. Need some inspiration? Try these five-minute solutions and see if you can incorporate a few of them into your chaotic days:

- Stretch
- Breathe
- Hug
- Voxer or text a friend
- Lie on the floor in a full body stretch with your eyes closed
- Splash your face with cold water

- Give your face a steam bath while cooking that pasta
- Dance to a favorite song
- Run around your house a few times
- Bust out a quick round of jumping jacks
- Jump on a trampoline for a few minutes
- Light a candle
- Savor a piece of dark chocolate
- Journal your feelings
- Enjoy a cup of tea

When I'm feeling overwhelmed, I often turn to baking. There's something about the soothing ritual of stirring together ingredients that is comforting in my times of stress. This is a go-to, one-pot, easy, "healthy-ish" blueberry coffee cake that is always a crowd-pleaser, and it goes great with that cup of tea.

Blueberry Coffee Cake

- 3 cups all-purpose flour
- 2 tsp baking powder
- 1 tsp baking soda
- 1 tsp salt
- 2 sticks of butter (1 cup)
- 1 1/2 cups sugar or 3/4 cup maple syrup
- 3 large eggs
- 16 oz plain yogurt
- 2 cups frozen blueberries

Topping

- 2/3 cup brown sugar
- 1/2 cup sugar
- 2 tsp cinnamon
- 1 tsp vanilla

Preheat the oven to 375º F. Combine flour, baking powder, baking soda, and salt in a small bowl. Set aside. Beat the butter and sugar together. Add the eggs to the butter and sugar, one at a time. Gradually add the other mixed dry ingredients and then the yogurt. Carefully fold in the blueberries. Pour into a greased and floured 9 x 13 pan. Mix the topping ingredients together and crumble over the top. Bake for 30–40 minutes, until a toothpick comes out clean.

Bedtime

We recently pulled the trigger and did a thing. Kind of a taboo thing. Ryan and I each purchased our own bed. Yep, you read that correctly. We don't sleep together anymore—at least, not in the same bed. It took ten years to get to the point of admitting that sleeping together was detrimental to many aspects of our life, including our mental health, physical health, anxiety levels, and stress management. Sleep is so important for self-care and even more so for couple care when you're raising children and one with special needs who demands to have his needs met at the crack of dawn. We desperately needed our rest to function optimally.

We tried everything. We really did. We bought an expensive Tempur-Pedic® mattress, which I hated. We purchased numerous toppers—some fluffy, some hard as a rock, some in between, all a waste of money. Our latest topper was ruined after a particularly tumultuous night of sleep where I tossed and turned, unable to get comfortable due to my aching hips; and as soon as the sun rose the next morning, I ripped it off our bed and stuffed it into the linen closet. Those of you who are familiar with the sheer magnitude of a king size foam topper can appreciate the strength it took to maneuver this thing into a small space, but adrenaline was pumping, and I was determined to not sleep another night on that particular monstrosity.

Anyway, a few months later we heard a "drip, drip, drip" from the back of that linen closet and lo and behold, we discovered a leak originating from the upstairs shower. This drip had been going for quite some time, and this expensive topper was now covered in mold.

After hauling the ruined topper to the trash, Ryan and I had a heart-to-heart about our sleeping arrangement. Now, to be completely transparent, I've suggested separate beds for years. I like the firmest, hardest, cheapest mattress money can buy. I know, weird, but if there's any hint of softness or squishiness, I'm toast. I will not sleep, and my hips will ache all night long. Ryan loves Tempur-Pedic®, and if he sleeps on a hard, cheap mattress, his shoulder will ache, and he will toss and turn. And then if my restless leg syndrome kicks in or perimenopausal hormones . . . well, you get the point. We both toss and turn a lot and keep each other awake, which led to the conversation on the edge of the bed.

"Honey," I said hesitantly, "I love you dearly, but I really don't want to sleep with you anymore."

"I know," he agreed. "It's probably time to look at separate beds, but," he continued, "I do have one stipulation."

"What?" I asked, fairly certain it was going to have to do with sex.

"I want to cuddle in one of our beds until the lights go out, and then we can move to our separate spaces."

"Deal," I agreed.

We purchased two queen beds, set them up smack dab next to each other, bought matching comforters, Ryan constructed a custom-size headboard to accommodate our strange solution, and it has been life changing. We can toss and turn to our heart's delight and not worry about waking the other one up. I can sprawl out my long legs and hoard the blankets because they're all mine! And he can do the same. Honestly, the only thing that really held us back for years was a fear over societal expectations—*heavens, what would people think?*

I guess eleven years into marriage, we are over what people think and much more concerned with getting a good night's sleep (and I bet a bunch of you are thinking, *hmmm, that might be something we need to think about,* right?).

Ryan's Take

Jess and I have never been good sleepers, and we are constantly searching for ways to improve our rest. And when I say "we," I mean Jess shares her latest findings of how and why we don't sleep and what we should try next. I am more of a "grin and bear it" kind of guy; Jess sees a problem and searches the world to solve it. I love that about her. I never had structured sleep habits before I met her, but she did, and if I wanted to sleep in the same room as my bride, I needed to adjust. I'm flexible, which makes it fairly easy to change my habits as long as I'm willing. Jess had been passively telling me that she did not want to sleep in the same bed with me to avoid hurting my feelings, even though she knew we would both benefit. Turns out, she was right; and truth be told, she usually is (but don't tell her I said that). Sleeping in separate beds like our grandparents did made me feel old. She did mention this subject numerous times in our marriage, but she typically got an eye roll and an under-the-breath grunt that meant I was not willing to consider it. But once she gets something in her head, I've learned to listen sooner rather than later. She needed something to change and needed me to recognize that our current sleeping arrangement wasn't working. We did finally have the discussion, and after realizing my biggest concern really only involved what other people thought, we went for it. She helped me understand what she was feeling and reminded me how much better we sleep on vacation when there are two beds (and no kids, which I'm sure helps). And you know, now that we have our two beds, side by side, I definitely sleep better knowing that my constant tossing and turning isn't keeping her awake, and vice versa. Maybe those "old people" who typically stayed married fifty-plus years learned early on that it doesn't matter what outsiders think. You do what's best for your marriage. To those wondering how it has affected our intimacy, I'll say this: when my wife gets enough sleep, she is happier and has a lot more energy for extracurriculars in the bedroom—and for ideas like growing her own vineyard.

Pruning for Self-Care

When we lived on our rural homestead, I had a brilliant idea—of course I did. I have always taken great pleasure in a nice glass of cold chardonnay, and now that we owned thirty acres of hills, I thought, *Why don't we plant chardonnay grapes and make wine?*

I immediately hopped on eBay and found what I was looking for—a cluster of grapevines ready to be planted in our red southern dirt. I placed the order and eagerly awaited their arrival—with visions of my basement shelves lined with bottles of chardonnay, made from my own two hands and from the grapes that had come straight from our land. Never mind that *no one* has ever grown chardonnay grapes in southern US soil, as they are typically grown in climates like Michigan or Northern California because it's the cooler weather that gives them that crisp buttery taste, or so I've been told.

But—I was not to be deterred. I was determined to grow grapes and make wine, by golly.

The grapes arrived, and Ryan and I put their tender root systems into the ground.

"Wow!" I exclaimed about thirty minutes into attempting to entrench a shovel into the hard red dry dirt that was to become my sweet little chardonnay vines' new home. "This isn't easy!"

"I told you," my husband replied. "Tennessee isn't exactly known for their vineyards, and there's probably a reason for that." He winked, slightly annoyed, but he understood that this meant a lot to me, and he's a trooper like that.

We continued working, and within a few hours those tender vines were planted.

The first year, nothing.

The second year, nothing.

The third year, I was so excited to see tons of growth! Twisty vine leaves going crazy! So crazy that my husband had to tie them up on wires!

"Yay! It looks like we might see a few grapes this year!" I said, enthralled over the prospect of finally fulfilling my dream of making homemade wine.

"Nope," my husband replied. "Not this year. This year we'll have to prune these vines back so that next year we can enjoy our harvest."

"WHAT?! Why?!" I wailed. "It looks so promising right now!"

"I know, babe, but that's what we have to do to ensure the best harvest. You have to prune to create room for real growth. If we leave the branches the way they are this year, sure, we'll see a grape here or there; but if we prune them this year, next year you'll be able to reap a harvest!"

"Fine," I agreed, disappointed but willing to take him at his word.

That spring we did indeed prune those branches. It hurt to see all that potential being hauled off to the burn pile, but I was excited to see what the next spring would bring, hopeful that my dreams of wine making were only a few months away!

Even the best laid plans can go awry. That fall, I heard, "Jess, they want to schedule a PET scan. They think it might be cancer."

Fear and uncertainty hung in the air as we contemplated our life that had become overwhelming and had led to Ryan's health issues. For the past six years he had single-handedly renovated our homestead, a sprawling 6,000 square foot home that was in dire need of everything when we purchased it, in addition to our daily life and work, which were hectic!

We were so overwhelmed we couldn't see straight. After receiving the news that all was clear on the scan (Praise the Lord!), we knew something had to give, or the next scare might not turn out as positively. It was really that simple; so, we evaluated our lives. What could we say no to? And what needed pruning? After a season of prayer, we knew that it was time to say goodbye to our beautiful homestead in rural Tennessee and goodbye to the grapevines. Goodbye to my dreams of making homemade chardonnay.

We packed up what once was our dream life, and by Christmas that year, we found a home near Nashville, and we moved. Although I never got to see a single grape on those grapevines, a student of mine gifted me with something special on my last day teaching. He and his grandfather made homemade wine from the muscadine grapes—apparently those do well in the South—and he brought me a bottle.

We pruned what wasn't working to make room for something that might. We said no to rural life in order to say yes to us.

Is there something affecting your mental, physical, or spiritual health? Pick up those shears and prune it. It will sting at first, but it's worth it. Every ounce of my being was sad to say goodbye to rural life; but in saying goodbye, I said yes to my husband's and family's well-being.

NOTES

[1] "Caring for the Caregiver," National Alliance for Caregiving, accessed July 15, 2022, https://www.caregiving.org/resources/caregiver-health/.

[2] Preetha Anand et al., "Cancer Is a Preventable Disease That Requires Major Lifestyle Changes," *Pharmaceutical Research* 25, no. 9 (Sep. 2008): 2,097–116, accessed July 15, 2022, https://www.ncbi.nlm.nih.gov/pmc/articles/PMC2515569/.

[3] National Alliance for Caregiving in collaboration with AARP, "Caregivers of Children: A Focused Look at Those Caring for a Child with Special Needs under the Age of 18," AARP, November 2009, accessed July 15, 2022, https://www.aarp.org/content/dam/aarp/research/surveys_statistics/general/2011/caregiving-09-children.doi.10.26419%252Fres.00062.007.pdf.

2

INTIMACY

What This Word Means and Why It's Vital for a Thriving Relationship

What is intimacy? Is it touching? Or a special feeling when you're with someone? A feeling of romance, perhaps? And, how can we cultivate more intimacy in our relationships? What value does it bring to a marriage?

Collins English Dictionary defines *intimacy* as "a close, familiar, and usually affectionate or loving personal relationship with another person or group."[1]

And that's a nice definition, but what I've observed from many marriages is that instead of a loving relationship, a disdain slowly arises after many years together. This sadly seems to be the status quo, rather than being the exception to the rule, as seen in the divorce rates that linger at around 44 percent for first marriages—the closeness that should occur when two people vow to love, honor, and cherish one another until death do them part seems to dissipate over time.

How do we prevent this nasty trend from occurring in our marriage? Is there a magic formula to circumvent this from happening? How do some couples—you know the ones I'm referring to, those holding hands while crossing the street or ending every phone call with "I love you"—manage to grow closer with time while others shrink away in disgust as the years go by?

Admittedly, many opportunities vie for our attention these days—cell phones, busy schedules, children, soccer games, and church activities to name a few—but true intimacy is born from a concerted desire to say no when many of these good activities beckon. True intimacy makes the choice to cultivate a relationship with the one we love. We cannot grow our relationships without dedicated time together—conversing, laughing, and exploring how we could do better. True intimacy also consists of honestly facing our struggles, fears, and addictions by admitting our shortcomings and pulling these harmful weeds from our relationship. Once the weeds are pulled, intimacy can grow because we're no longer hiding from each other. When our true selves are laid bare and our spouse still loves and accepts us despite our sinful nature, true intimate freedom is found. This is the sweet spot where we can uninhibitedly focus on the present and move forward into a future with the one we love. But how do we change? How we speak to each other is a great place to start; and believe me, I have plenty of experience with this one.

A gentle answer turns away wrath, but a harsh word stirs up anger. (Prov. 15:1)

Words That Wound

I have historically used words, particularly harsh words, as a form of armor. I'm a writer and a woman. This potentially lethal combination can sometimes lead to ugly accusations and statements flying about haphazardly. Words that have the ability to destroy intimacy with my husband. Sometimes what I've said has haunted me for years after I've allowed the words to exit my mouth. I'm not proud of this trait and abhor the fact that I can't simply stop myself through pure will and determination. Yes, I've become more gracious and self-controlled, but when the gloves come out or I feel like I'm not being heard, my first area of ammunition is slashing and dashing with my tongue.

There is an immense amount of power in the words we use to speak to our spouses, and I've learned, over time, that it is a choice. It's a honed skill to not spout off in anger or to walk away if need be. Our words also have the power to speak into existence our perspective of a situation—including our perspective of our relationship.

We either build the life we want with our words, or we destroy our life. Death and life are in the power of the tongue (Prov. 18:21). If we constantly tell our girlfriends what a slimeball, good-for-nothing husband we have, we will turn him into exactly that. If instead we praise our man and thank him for working so hard for the family, we will inspire our husbands who will move mountains on our behalf!

I heard a story once that has really stuck with me through the years. This story is about a woman who attended a dinner party with her husband who happened to be the mayor. At this party, they ran into an old boyfriend of hers who had spent his life as a plumber. Her husband, the mayor, commented, "Aren't you glad you married me, instead of him? He became a plumber, and I'm the mayor!" She grinned and replied, "If I had married him, he would have been mayor." I love this story. Not so much because I do everything perfectly, and my husband is the most blessed man on the planet because he married me, but because it speaks the truth about the spousal relationship. If we believe in one another, we can rise to our full potential! I know this to be true of my relationship with Ryan. He has always had my back and believed in my ability to become an author and operate a nonprofit. He has never once questioned my talents or drive—although he does occasionally suggest that I slow down a bit. His words of encouragement have helped shape the woman I am today.

Words have the ability to cultivate intimacy—even words that are difficult to hear. Through complete vulnerability, we can admit our struggles and then move forward in true intimacy with one another. One of the hardest seasons of my life was when Ryan asked me to walk alongside him and keep him accountable concerning a lifelong struggle with a specific sin. By allowing me to partner with him through this dark period of life, we were able to rise above the pain and become more united and stronger together; but it was hard. Our intimacy was restored and elevated through his honest admission and my eventual forgiveness. I believe most spouses yearn for this deep well of intimacy, but it's not easy and will require the choice to build the marriage on respect and positivity rather than disdain and anger.

One last thought: our Savior understood the power of words—so much so that he promised that one day we would stand in judgment before him and give an account of every word we spoke on earth. In Matthew 12:35-37, Jesus states:

> A good man brings good things out of the good stored
> up in him, and an evil man brings evil things out of
> the evil stored up in him. But I tell you that everyone
> will have to give account on the day of judgment for

every empty word they have spoken. For by your words
you will be acquitted, and by your words you will
be condemned.

That's quite the promise. May we all stand acquitted before our
spouses and before our Lord.

See Me

"Would you please put your phone away?" My husband glanced at
me where I sat comfortably in the passenger seat of his truck as we
meandered down the road in search of our date night destination.

"What?" I hardly glanced up, clearly engrossed in what Susan
had to say on Facebook.

"Put your phone away," he requested again. "I want to spend
time with you on our date. I don't go on dates so I can watch you
looking at your phone."

"Honey," I explained, "I have to wrap up this post, and then I
promise I'll put it away."

He rolled his eyes, clearly annoyed.

"Fine," I said, returning the annoyance. "I'll finish later." And
with that statement, the phone went into the console, and we sat
together in silence.

This is a struggle I have.

Screen time, or more specifically social media time, is my
drug of choice and such an easy drug to rationalize in my line
of work. Screen time is marketing time or advocating time or
making a difference in the world time, and we sure need more
people to do this, right? Screen time is where Jess is patted on
the back and affirmed for her accomplishments, whereas Mom
time is where Jess is told dinner sucks and the rules suck and my
whole life sucks, and it's all mom's fault! Screen time is an easy and
lazy way to zone out as the kids are yelling "Mom! Mom! Mom!"

for the hundredth time or arguing with one another or as Lucas screams or I sit beside him and try to determine, yet again, what my nonverbal child is requesting. Screen time numbs the chaos rather than diving into the nitty-gritty and figuring out how to soothe the angst.

I know I'm not alone in this struggle, but there are always consequences to our decisions, right? I know when I'm zoned out a bit too often my family suffers. They get restless and angry when Mom isn't paying attention, and don't we all? I get irritated when I'm out for dinner with a friend, and she can't stop looking at her phone. It makes me feel unimportant, and I wonder why we're together in the first place if her online community is so much more interesting.

My type A self is really proficient at implementing screen time boundaries for the family, but I'm not so great at implementing them for myself. It's been a process, but I've landed on a few tried-and-true solutions that help combat the addictive nature of social media and restore intimacy with my husband and family. Maybe a couple of these will be helpful for you too.

First, no phones at the dinner table. Pretty simple, or at least it should be. Dinnertime is for catching up on the day, and if you're the beloved youngest child, it's for sharing your thoughts about how disgusting the meal tastes.

Second, Ryan and I put our phones to bed at 8:00 p.m. and not in our bedroom! We have a centrally located charging station, and the expectation is that everyone's phone and/or device is charging there before bedtime.

Third, I've implemented a rule that includes no social media apps being allowed on my phone. I used to have all the normal ones—Facebook, Instagram, and Pinterest—and I'd find myself on them in an everyday situation like pumping gas. Apparently, boredom hit in those thirty seconds, and I had to whip out my phone and see what happened on Facebook. Or let's say I was sitting on a bench at the park with my kids. Rather than interacting or being at peace with my thoughts, out came Instagram because, of course, something life-changing had to be occurring that I couldn't miss out on . . . or could I? That became the question that led to the decision to take social media off my phone.

The experts claim this current generation lacks imagination because they never allow themselves to be bored due to the constant stimulation of devices, and it's true! Lately, I've started my morning walks without any devices and half of this book has come to me as I've allowed my brain the freedom to breathe, wander, and think rather than stuffing it full of random thoughts and opinions from online strangers. Imagine all the amazing ideas that haven't been implemented because people are so preoccupied with social media!

I also have unfollowed (not unfriended but unfollowed) almost everyone in my Facebook feed. This action put a major damper on my scrolling because I'm simply not seeing updates. If a person comes to mind, I will meander on over to their page and see how they are and often leave a comment and maybe a short prayer, but there's no reason to be constantly distracted and bombarded by what Susie ate for lunch or what Tom said about the current political administration.

These are choices.

My choices.

Finally, my former pastor, a sage man whom I admire, had this to say when asked how he manages to avoid the social media trap as a well-known author, podcaster, and speaker: "I don't post anything that's not about the work."

I thought, *That is wise advice.* Yes, of course, I'm going to take advantage of the free marketing social media offers; but as a writer and advocate, my posts should point back to the creative work

I've been called to accomplish: writing, advocacy, and making a difference in the lives of caregivers. My posts should simply be about advancement toward a better world and bringing glory to my Father in Heaven. His advice has become my barometer; is this about the work or is it about your ego? It's that simple. I had to get a grip on what held my soul captive, and managing this entanglement was instrumental in my mental and physical well-being and in the intimacy within my relationships.

No one wants to feel like an electronic device is more important than an actual human relationship, and any vice or addiction will hinder growth in intimacy. Consider what keeps you from freedom and then make a plan to release yourself from the grip of addiction. Your spouse will thank you for it.

See Me Too

It's human nature to desire being truly seen and needed—especially in our most intimate relationships. I want my family to see how hard my life can be and offer help. I want my closest friends to recognize that it is a lot easier if they visit me because of special-needs hurdles, and I want my husband to see when I'm exhausted and need a break.

I was recently interviewed for a prominent podcast and one of the questions asked was, "Jess, you and Ryan have such busy lives as caregivers to eight children and, additionally, a seventeen-year-old child who needs total care for the rest of his life. How do you manage caregiver burnout?"

It took me a moment to gather my thoughts, and I realized, "Ryan and I have never suffered from burnout at the same time"— thankfully! We've never even been sick at the same time. Yes, he's gotten the flu a time or two, and I immediately think, *No, no, no, no! We cannot both go down! Who will steer this ship?!* But one of us is always fully recovered before the other finally goes down, probably because our immune systems are shot after being single parents. I do believe this is the Lord's grace over our family because until recently, there truly was not a backup plan if we both went down. The same has been true in our relationship with caregiver burnout. We've never both been maxed out at the same time, and we've been honest with one another when we feel ourselves entering that place of no return—that panicky, stressed-out, heart-racing place, which we've been familiar with in the past.

After our move to Michigan, Ryan was spent. Flat out, on his back, exhausted. He had traveled back and forth from Tennessee numerous times during the month of May to single-handedly move our family, and by the time he landed in the Mitten for good, he was cooked well-done. One of his favorite pastimes is golf, and he sat me down after the move and said, "Honey, I'm exhausted and need some me time. What works for you if I want to golf for a few hours in the next week?"

Initially, I became a bit resentful and replied, "Nine or eighteen holes?" I knew that he desired eighteen, but I also knew that the amount of time it takes to golf eighteen holes would require me to solo parent for about five hours. I was not excited about doing this on the weekend with six restless children, which can make it nearly impossible to leave the house, our temporary home that, yes, I was grateful for, but that was beginning to feel a bit like a tomb.

However, I took a deep breath and realized I've had the same conversation with him numerous times as I've asked for a few hours to enjoy time with a girlfriend or a massage, and he has never turned me down.

"Sure, that'll be good for you," I replied. "You deserve it."

I wasn't fully on board even as I said yes, but I set aside my pride and agenda in order to gift my husband some self-care; and that's what it is, right? We love our spouses and gift them with self-care. Not a gift that says *now you owe me*, but a gift of grace. A gift with zero strings attached. A gift that acknowledges their needs before our own.

How can you honor your spouse's need for self-care in the next couple of weeks? Is this a possibility? Broach the subject and watch how your husband or wife lights up as you give them an opportunity to breathe—and bonus, you will reap the benefits of further intimacy by allowing your spouse to feel seen and known.

Finding Your Voice

Our daughter Annabelle makes me laugh. As I write this book, she is an extremely confident six-year-old. I don't know if this is a result of being the youngest of eight children or learning from her mother, who has also become quite confident in her older years, but this child does not mince words. If she wants something, she flat-out says it, like the other day when she turned to her little posse of friends, put her hands on her hips, and declared, "I'm done playing today. It's time for you to go home."

Can you imagine if we were that straightforward as adults? Imagine saying to your spouse or friend, "You know, I'm tired. I'm done being on this committee." Or, "No, I don't want to go out for dinner because this relationship makes me feel bad about myself." Or, "I'm not going to the potluck because I'd rather spend a quiet evening at home with my family." Rude? Maybe a little. Honest? Absolutely. Desperately needed in our world? Probably!

My first husband, Jason, and I were both skillful in truth-telling, and because we were so proficient at not being passive, we often found ourselves in loud, heated arguments during the first years of marital bliss. I remember one specific discussion, probably about money, where we flung rounds of spiteful accusations, statements that weren't true but blades nonetheless that would be driven deeply into the heart of the one we had vowed to love, honor, and cherish till death do us part. We flung these daggers for about an hour before Jason stormed out of the house, and I locked the doors. I remember peering out of the living room window at my husband sitting on the front porch, head between his hands, in prayer. I did eventually let him back into the house, and those young immature days of spouting off whatever thoughts landed in our minds were eventually replaced with respect and holding our tongues as real-life challenges such as special needs and cancer taught us that life is short and to value the time we had with one another.

My marriage with Ryan is different. Ryan is passive and will do anything to avoid confrontation. He is a peacemaker through and through. This was an interesting personality trait to encounter because I was used to a man speaking his mind. In my new marriage, I would suggest something, and the suggestion was met with passive agreement. I thought, *Gosh, this is wonderful! My husband agrees with everything!*

And he did in those early years! Or at least he pretended to.

Fast forward to present life and a recent scenario that should have been nothing. Really, a completely absurd fight.

Let me paint the scene.

We were living life in our double-wide while we waited for our house to be completed. I have absolutely nothing against double-wides. I lived in one during my first marriage to Jason; however, a double-wide with six children and autism and thin walls can create an intense situation quickly.

Here we were, living in our temporary home and needing to be aware and respectful of the fact that we were together in very tight quarters. And I was aware and respectful when I awoke early to enjoy some quiet time and coffee before the rest of the household came alive with loud chaos.

I typically wake up around 6:30–7:00 a.m. and quietly open the bedroom door and tiptoe out to the kitchen, turn the coffee machine on, and make my way to my favorite comfy chair to scroll through the morning news and read my devotions. I was usually granted about an hour before the rest of the house would begin to stir—and by "stir" I mean literally. Hang on . . .

Around 7:30 my husband usually emerged and not quietly. He flung open the creaking door, stomped out to the kitchen, poured himself a cup of coffee, added a few drops of honey, and then loudly clanged the silver spoon against the ceramic coffee cup for what seemed to be an eternity. I don't know if he was sounding the alarm for the rest of the family, but this simple act drove me batty. It really set me off on the wrong foot most days and disrupted my reading because now I was obsessively worried that my husband had woken the rest of the crew.

Now, younger Jessica would have spouted off her mouth and put her husband in his place. Younger Jessica has learned a thing or two in her older age.

I held my tongue, but still, this daily practice of his became like fingernails grating against a chalkboard. After a few days of enduring this obnoxious behavior, I knew I had to say something, but I held off until the evening.

Once we were in bed, I turned to my husband and kindly said, "In the morning, when you get up, it really disrupts my peace, and I think wakes some of the kids up, when you stir the honey in your coffee cup."

"Are you serious?" he scoffed, obviously irritated.

Maybe I shouldn't have brought it up right before bed, but I felt passionately that I needed to speak my truth gracefully before the next morning and without instigating a full-blown argument over a stupid cup of coffee.

Ryan's statement was a big deal from my peacemaker husband, a personality trait that often led to discomfort with communication, especially confrontational communication. However, he's learned that to further the intimacy in our relationship, he needs to voice his concerns—even if they might make the marital situation less than peaceful for a period of time with his headstrong wife.

It was an uncomfortable conversation but one that opened the door to air more irritations that had been simmering below the surface, irritations that could have festered and put a damper on our intimacy over the long run. As we talked, I discovered Ryan would rather not have uncomfortable conversations right before bedtime because it destroys his peace, and then he can't sleep. He learned that my peace in the morning is a nonnegotiable and is required to start my day on the right track.

When all was said and done, he kissed me goodnight and said, "Thanks for letting me know, and I promise I'll try to be more respectful of the situation tomorrow morning."

"Perfect," I said, returning his smooch before rolling over and dozing off to a peaceful sleep because, thankfully, our conversation had not led to anything full-blown.

I have learned to hold space for Ryan when he asks to talk about something sensitive, and by this I mean I don't immediately try to bulldoze him with words—something with which my sinful nature struggles. Words that wound can often be related to an issue in the marriage, or they may be totally unrelated and our spouse becomes a punching bag for something bigger we're dealing with. Something that may leave us feeling out of control as I did when I launched into a tirade about an old, nasty desk my husband left in our front yard.

Releasing Control

One peaceful night as Ryan sat in front of the TV watching *River Monsters*, I began to nag him about the old, broken-down desk in our front yard that he used as a support system for his wood-working hobby. I walked up and down the hallways of our house, muttering under my breath, hoping to catch his ear, but he was really engrossed in what he was watching or he had become really adept at tuning out his wife.

I walked and muttered and kicked a ratty stuffed bunny into the corner.

"I can't stand how redneck we look with all that trash in the yard," I huffed and puffed, and what I really meant was I couldn't stand how redneck my husband seemed to be at times.

I glanced out the front window at the disheveled sight before me. A few years prior, we had purchased thirty acres of God's beautiful Southern country, and how did my husband go about tending this beautiful land of ours? He littered it with "treasures" he either found or bought or were given to him, including a weather-beaten, rusted-down desk that he took from an old barn he helped demolish in exchange for the paraphernalia inside. Those treasures had to go somewhere, and that somewhere became my front yard.

The sight of this desk not only irritated me; it grated my very last nerve on this particular day. I couldn't understand why he wouldn't move it someplace where it wouldn't be such an eye sore. I mean, really; did it have to be the first thing people noticed as they drove up our driveway? Or maybe that wasn't fair. Perhaps the first thing they noticed was the broken washing machine next to it. I rolled my eyes for my own satisfaction.

I said to him, louder this time, "Darling husband, that desk is so ugly, and it makes us look like we don't care about cleanliness or order or even patriotism! Or that we're too lazy to bring the trash to the dump. It looks tacky, and it doesn't reflect well on me as the wife and mother running our home because Southern women generally have their homes in order."

He glanced my way, slightly annoyed that I was interrupting his show but said nothing.

"Honey, do you understand what I'm saying?" I continued, not at all deterred by his lack of enthusiasm regarding the conversation. "Southern women take care of their yards. Their porches are immaculate with big, beautiful pots overflowing with flowers, and they monogram their front doors, and people oohh and ahhh over the beauty that these women present through their homes. The Ronnes are the opposite—people drive up to our house, and they see this ugly, old, broken desk in our front yard, and it doesn't reflect well on my transplanted Southern homemaking abilities. I would move it if I could!" I shouted.

Silence.

"It's too heavy to move, but I can burn it!" I threatened.

"Don't burn the desk," he calmly replied, looking intently into the madness staring back at him.

"Fine," I agreed. "I won't burn the desk, but we need to come up with a solution soon."

I left the room and let my frustration hang thickly in the air.

I considered what was really going on in my heart. Was it truly about the desk? Or was there something deeper at play?

Two days later I received a text. "We lost him."

A good friend's brother-in-law unexpectedly died after only a few short months of fighting cancer. He was in his forties. His wife stepped away from his sickbed, and in that instant, he left earth. I had only made two freezer meals for the family. His widow hadn't even had the opportunity to get sick of freezer burned casseroles before she lost her husband.

More fatherless children. Children like mine had once been. Another widow with a bleeding heart as mine had once ached.

Beastly cancer always getting the best of people.

People dying; people hurting; people in hospitals; children, widows, widowers left in the wake; and old desks left in front yards. All of it broken.

God, why can't he just move that stupid desk?!
Something I could control.
Something we could control.
Something that doesn't really matter.

Like my own frantic actions in 2010 as I angrily attempted to rip every single weed out of a flower garden with tears streaming down my face. Every single weed representing a cancer cell. Every single weed representing a perception of control.

But only a perception.

Always a perception and nothing more.

The old hymn "My Hope Is Built on Nothing Less" was playing in the background as I gently stirred the pea soup simmering away on the stove for that evening's dinner.

I got this, a voice whispered.

It's not the desk.

It's not cancer.

It's not even your husband's stubborn ways.

I got this, the voice whispered again.

I've got cancer.

I've got your husband.

I've got your anger.

I even have your perception of control.

I've got it all in the palm of my hand.

I awoke the next morning and glanced out the window. The desk had been moved into the barn and someone came to pick up the washing machine later that day, convinced they could fix it. I was thrilled that it was now another wife's problem and no longer mine.

My hope is built on nothing less than Jesus' blood and righteousness. I dare not trust the sweetest frame, but wholly lean on Jesus' name. On Christ, the solid rock, I stand: all other ground is sinking sand; all other ground is sinking sand.[2]

How about you? Do you use words to harm? Or are you more like my husband who doesn't use enough words, which can also harm a relationship? For us, calling a time-out has been a beneficial practice because neither of us can see straight in the middle of a heated argument. This time allows us to consider how maybe what we're upset about isn't really the issue. It also gives us the space we need to calm down, take a deep breath, maybe talk to the Lord, and then come back together in a safer space to work toward a resolution that will restore our relationship and our intimacy with one another.

Pea Soup

I made this soup as I stewed about that old desk. Most versions of pea soup are made with a ham hock, and I do that sometimes, but this version is made with bacon and bone broth, which is just as tasty. Enjoy.

- 1 16 oz package of bacon
- 1 small onion, chopped
- 4 carrots, chopped
- 3 celery stalks, chopped
- 2 garlic cloves, peeled and minced
- About 64 oz bone broth
- Salt and pepper to taste
- 2 cups split peas soaked overnight

In a large stockpot or Dutch oven, cook the bacon, then remove and crumble it, but leave the drippings in the pot. Sauté the onion, garlic, celery, and carrots in the drippings for a few minutes (be careful not to burn the garlic!). Drain the peas, then add them and broth. Bring to a simmer, cover, and cook for two to three hours (or longer if peas aren't soft). Stir occasionally. When peas are soft, add bacon bits, and salt and pepper to taste.

• •

Spring Walks—Dealing with Your Anger

I usually walk with Ryan first thing in the morning; but often after lunch, I'll walk again by myself to take a break. On these walks of solitude, I often invite Jesus to tag along.

One beautiful sunny day, I hadn't slept well the night before. Mainly the events of the world—political and social unrest—had caused a lot of anger in my spirit, and I tossed and turned throughout the night, playing and replaying worst-case scenarios about the future of my family. What if the world came to an abrupt end and we had to fend for ourselves, like against the walking dead? How would I do this with Lucas who can't walk? How would we survive? Yes, these were the thoughts I fell asleep to; not the best scenarios to be running through my mind at bedtime. I tried to pray, but the thoughts continued, and I was angry. Angry that I didn't have the self-discipline to turn off the news, angry that my fears were getting the best of me, angry that my husband still hadn't moved all the junk in our yard, and angry that Jesus seemed to be oblivious to everything going on in the world! I wasn't sure that he understood exactly how dire the situation was here on earth, and I thought I should be the one to break it to him. I said to him, "Lord, as a culture, we are so angry. Anger bubbles beneath the surface in our homes and churches, and our screens; our world-wide webs are the worst! Here we see an avalanche of righteous indignation that covers humanity with red hot lava and makes us anxious as we move throughout our chaotic lives. Oh yes, we have flaming hot, angry opinions, and it erodes the intimacy in our relationships."

I said this to him and then continued with my explanations:

We hurl rocks from our self-righteous perches behind brightly lit screens; the hefty, tyrannical boulders that fall heavy upon seemingly invisible and invincible souls.

We hurl until our shoulders ache and our hearts are muddied and black, and we are unable to find joy in anything anymore.

We hurl until Stephen is finally dead beneath the weight of our words.

And these angry words, Lord, leave in their wake empty little crevices, and we thrive on the power we have through our anger. These holes we create in people's souls overflow with insecurities and pain, and we find ourselves back in Eden beneath the tree of despair, back where we are caught holding the forbidden and asking ourselves: *Why must we always return to the tree?! How do we fix it, Lord?*

I prayed as the tears trickled down my face, hidden by the oversized sunglasses perched high upon my nose. How do we remedy such an expansive brokenness? How do we set aside our anger and return to intimate communion with one another?

Jesus didn't have much to say, and so I slowly trudged up the last hill and veered into my husband's garden to see if I could possibly scrounge up one or two remaining tomatoes, the delicious fruit of his labor I'd been enjoying all summer.

I meandered through the garden and noticed that the plants hung limp, their life long gone and instead replaced with brittle branches. A few stubborn stalks held remnants of rotten fruit, fruit that didn't ripen in time or fruit mauled by creatures great and small, and it occurred to me that the answer to most of my questions included a simple, time-honored truth found in Scripture: We are to bear fruit. Period.

We who walk with Christ, our job is to bear fruit—fruit that will be life nourishing to many, and sometimes even life saving for a few. Not all of us will have the best or the prettiest fruit to bear at the stage we're at in life, but it is still our duty to give what we have, however that looks in this moment. Wherever we are in the ripening process of "becoming more like him," we should offer what we have to the weary world, including our families and spouses. He commands this of us. Offer our kindness, patience, steadfastness, and faithfulness and respond in love, gentleness, and self-control whenever possible.

This might include hitting the delete button when the perfect, angry barrage of words easily fires off the keyboard in response to something we don't agree with. That's fruit. Or perhaps it's displaying joy in the midst of sleep deprivation and patiently explaining to our children how to complete their tasks yet again. More fruit. Or considering it "pure joy" to change another diaper for a child with profound special needs, viewing it through a lens of honor, rather than grief, as you care for someone who cannot care for themselves. Not fantastically impressive fruit by worldly standards, but holy fruit rendered in obedience to him. Or replying to your husband's snarky comment with grace rather than retorting in anger. That's hard fruit to give, isn't it?

Will you join me and give your fruit to the world, to your loved ones, and to your spouse? Jot down what that fruit is for your situation and how you can release it to bring greater intimacy into your relationships.

And remember that old desk that sat in our front yard and made me spew with righteous anger? A few months later, Ryan surprised me with an early birthday gift. He had secretly transformed that nasty old piece of junk into a beautiful writing desk where I sit today and type my stories. He presented me with his fruit. He looked past my anger and lent grace, and in doing so, he brought redemption and intimacy to a situation that could have been riddled with anger.

Vulnerable Moments

In 2021, our family made the difficult decision to uproot our lives yet again and move. In 2013, we had moved to Tennessee to pursue a dream of a simple life. We purchased a big, old, deserted house on thirty acres in need of total renovation, and we got to work. We poured our hearts and souls into this dream, and it was beautiful and life-giving—and then it wasn't anymore. As Lucas aged, it became difficult, isolating, and exhausting, and it caused health problems in Ryan and myself. So, we changed what wasn't working and moved toward Nashville. We thought an urban environment would provide the support and resources we needed for Lucas. What we discovered, instead, was that there are very few places in the world that provide what we need on a societal level. We decided to no longer put our hope in the government, which led to the decision to head home to Michigan where our friends and family would surround us and offer support when we needed it. This was a decision that was bathed in prayer before we bravely took the steps necessary to make it a reality. Moving day arrived in April, and it was time for me to move with Lucas and our fourteen-year-old daughter Mabel. We understood that moving our large crew and numerous belongings would take months, and we wanted to acclimate Lucas to his new school before the summer school program began—a huge perk and something we had missed in Tennessee.

Lucas thrives on structure, and when this routine is abruptly removed from his life, like it is every summer, the result is devastating for the entire family. He does not cognitively understand why he can't continue to go to school and will uncontrollably scream. Mabel also requested to join because she wanted to make new friends before heading off to high school the following year.

After a long day of driving, we landed in Michigan where the next couple of days were spent unpacking and getting settled before Ryan headed back to Tennessee with the rest of the family. The four days flew by, and it was time for him to leave. I was heartbroken. I knew it would be a difficult transition as we lived out of two states for the next month.

"Bye, honey," I whispered into his ear as I squeezed his neck tight. "Send me a message when you arrive home."

"Will do, babe. I love you," he replied and then closed the door to his truck.

"Bye!" We all waved until he was out of sight, and then I closed the patio door and reentered my eerily quiet home. It was now just the three of us, and I wasn't sure what to think of the silence. It was deafening.

I stayed busy to avoid thinking about the weeks I had to live without my better half. Eight hours passed, and I finally received the text I had been waiting for.

"Made it home safe and sound." I sat there and stared at my phone. I missed my husband so much, and it had only been eight hours! How was I going to make it a whole month? I wanted to text back and pour my heart out to him, tell him how much he meant to me and how grateful I was to have him as a partner in life; but I couldn't. I came up with every excuse: *I'm sure he's busy and doesn't want to hear a sappy message from his weepy wife. He wants you to be strong, and you can't be a big baby.* But what it really came down to and why I couldn't bring myself to text what I was feeling was that it would make me seem vulnerable.

I'm known as a strong woman who can handle quite a bit, and if I'm being honest, I kind of like being known as this type of person. Who wants to be known as needy or weepy? These aren't highly desirable traits, and they're definitely not ones I want to be associated with. I'm the "just keep livin'" girl, right? If I sent a weepy text, Ryan might think I'm not as strong as I pretend to be. I mulled over these thoughts for the next few hours, and then as I got ready for bed, I heard that still small voice: *Send the text. Your husband needs to know you miss him.* "Really, Lord?" I responded. I gave my whole litany of excuses, and all I heard back was, *Send the text.*

I sent the text, and Ryan's reply filled my heart with peace. "God's got us, honey. He's always had us."

He was right. The Lord would see us through this difficult time apart. My husband understood that he could never be enough for me and that I needed to find peace and comfort in my Heavenly Father's promise to never leave nor forsake me. It wasn't going to be easy, but what doesn't kill us makes us stronger, right? That month flew by, and we were reunited again before we knew it.

Do you need to open yourself up and be more vulnerable in your relationship? Remember, vulnerability grows intimacy. Do you need to tell your spouse I love you? Bust a move on him, perhaps? Plant a big kiss on her lips in a room full of people? What would make your spouse feel loved? Consider these questions, and then do it. I promise it will bring you closer together and strengthen the bond you already share.

Ignorance Is Not Bliss

I'm not a marriage expert and even in agreeing to write a book about marriage, my nerves began to pitter patter because it seems like the second you act like you have it all together in a particular area of life, that area has a tendency to fall apart. So, I'm not necessarily a marriage expert; instead, I'm a type A, black-and-white, perfectionist individual who strives wholeheartedly to give everything 100 percent, including my marriage. This type of personality has pros and cons, but my heart is usually in the right place. I believe many of us settle for mediocre in our relationships, and it's sad, especially when we could make a few changes that would transform our lives significantly.

Early on in my marriage to Ryan, I stumbled across a document on our computer—our shared computer that arrived from his previous life. Out of curiosity, I read it. It was sensitive in nature and had to do with Ryan's former life. When he arrived home, I explained that I had found this document. (I know y'all are dying to know the details, but they really aren't important.)

"Did you read it?" he asked defensively.

"Yes," I responded. "It was on our computer!"

It was my understanding that as a married woman, I had a right to look at whatever was in my house. That's how I operated in my previous marriage, and I assumed the same would be true in this marriage.

My first marriage involved former boyfriends and girlfriends. My current marriage involved former spouses and children. It's a fine line that Ryan and I are still navigating; but for us, the distinction doesn't *feel* different when talking about former flings or former spouses, regardless of how the world expects us to feel or act. But therein lies the question: Should aspects of our former life remain private? Even when it relates to our new spouse?

We brainstormed one evening about what might belong under the banner of privacy, and some observations included passwords, former pictures, love letters, documents, diaries, thoughts, computers, devices, Facebook pages, emails, cell phones, bank accounts, and dreams. The questions we repeatedly returned to included these: Where is the line? What constitutes healthy boundaries, and what constitutes crossing those boundaries? Where does maintaining oneness in marriage become a twisted spousal attempt to control the marriage or the person?

I am admittedly a somewhat nosy person who relishes the *feeling* of having control over situations. I think most women struggle here, particularly in regard to our emotional well-being, which includes our spouses and families. I have a need to know about a lot of things. I'm extremely curious. If I question something or an issue pops up about any topic of interest, I am immediately online researching and then sharing my knowledge with the family at the dinner table. The firstborns love it. The rest, I'm pretty sure, are bored to tears. My mother has informed me that as a little girl I once asked, "Do worms poop?" That sums it up. I'm still interested in the answer to that question. Do they?

I believe this personality trait has its strengths, like how I know quite a bit about a bunch of subjects, and obviously weaknesses, like mainly trust issues.

Ryan and I hardly knew each other when we got married, but we felt strongly that our marriage was God led and ordained. To this day, we don't regret getting married only four months after meeting. We were 100 percent committed and have seen and experienced wonderful blessings attached to our decision; but that decision was laced with colorful pasts that led to trust issues.

I don't trust easily to begin with; throw in former spouses and grief and three new children, and documents that were apparently off-limits on our shared computer, and my heart was struggling that first year of marriage. I wanted to know who this man was that I had married and devoured anything I could find about him. I quickly discovered that a personal hurdle to intimacy for me was that I was now living with and loving someone who didn't always resemble the perfect, missionary blogger I had fallen in love with. Shockingly, Ryan was human.

Many marriages are destroyed over secrets, and transparency is required to experience true intimacy. Husbands and wives who bury their heads in the sand—accepting the "ignorance is bliss" model, who don't want to know their spouse's innermost thoughts, don't want to know about exes they still talk to, don't want to know how much money was lost at the casino last week, or what the computer search history might reveal—risk losing true intimacy in their marriage. These inactions and refusal to face the problems contribute quickly to the erosion of intimacy and, ultimately, the marriage.

There is a difference between privacy and secrets.

Privacy is acceptable if it doesn't involve secrets. Having a dream is private unless there is a heart issue that comes into play. Let's say the dream is stemming from a secret life. For example, the wife who is chatting online with an ex-boyfriend, thinking about him constantly to the point where it seeps into her dream life, and now she's having sex dreams about a man who is not her husband.

What we feed our brains throughout the day will manifest in our dreams. There is not a one-size-fits-all answer for thoughts and dreams, but I trust that God will reveal whether it should be kept private because it would only hurt a spouse or whether it should be brought to the light because it's rooted in secrecy and sin. Evil breeds in secrecy, and true intimacy cannot thrive there. Respect and love die quickly where secrets fester.

I didn't initially trust Ryan with my heart. He came into our marriage with "his stuff," which included things he didn't necessarily want me to know about! I came into the marriage with "my stuff." We had very little that was "our stuff." Early on we threw away mementos that could have potentially hurt one another. I don't hold on to belongings to relive the glory days or whatever people do with former love letters or pictures. Ryan knew I was going to get rid of many of these items, and that was enough for him. He didn't ask for details, but he also trusted that I wasn't allowing myself to wallow in the what-ifs of the past. There were no secrets in destroying the mementos; however, there was privacy in what these items contained.

Communication about secrets can be painful, but communication is growth, and marriages without it will die, either physically or emotionally. God's standard of marriage is comparable to

Christ's relationship with his bride, the church, which involves our broken down, fragile, in-need-of-grace marriages that must come before the throne of God on a daily basis.

My husband is my best friend, and I want to know him in a deeper way than anyone else in the universe knows him. I want him to know me deeper than anyone has ever known me and still choose me—still love me, just like Christ does with my murky, nasty, ugliness brought to light, and he still chooses me; he still loves me. That's intimate oneness and leads to trust as we share our lives, including our fears, with one another.

> **TAKEAWAY**
> Secrecy hurts, hides, and destroys. Privacy respects, loves, and protects.

Sharing Your Fears

It was January 2018. We had recently moved from our rural home to our new urban home. Annabelle was four years old. My birth story with my youngest daughter was traumatic and involved numerous post-birth infections and scary results from a pap smear where I was told there were "irregular cells" and was advised to "make a follow-up appointment in six months."

Six months turned into four years because "ignorance is bliss" compounded with my fear of the medical community, which began when Lucas was diagnosed in utero and intensified after Jason's battle with cancer and culminated with my experiences with Annabelle. In my mind, doctors weren't safe. Doctors told you bad news, and then you usually died. With this mindset, I did what any sane, rational person would do when they heard the news that there were "irregular cells in their uterus": I simply avoided doctors.

After our move to Nashville, I discovered that Vanderbilt Hospital offered midwives, and that option felt safer than a doctor. I scheduled my post-op appointment—four years later. The morning arrived for my appointment, and I felt nauseous. The anxiety caused me to lose my appetite, which Ryan noticed and asked, "You okay, babe?"

"I feel sick to my stomach," I confessed. "I'm scared they're going to find something wrong."

I sat at the kitchen table while tears threatened to spill over. My husband was busy in the next room, nonchalantly paying bills. He had no idea the amount of anguish I felt. He knew I avoided the doctor like the plague, but because I don't let my vulnerability show, he didn't know the extent of anguish this appointment had put me in. I decided to be brave and ask if he'd accompany me. I knew he might think I was a giant baby, but at least I'd put it out there.

"Ryan," I quietly whispered, "I know this won't be at the top of your list of fun things to do today, but would you come with me? I'm scared that they're going to find something wrong."

"Sure," he replied.

Just sure. Not a long explanation of how I'd be fine or a litany of excuses for why he couldn't come or how it was time for me to grow up already—just sure. Plain and simple.

We arrived at the clinic and were ushered into the examination room where I answered a few questions, underwent an examination (as my husband held my hand and whispered that everything would be fine), and I was told that everything did, in fact, appear to be just fine. I was then escorted back out to the main lobby where we learned that we would have the results in a week or two.

And because I was such a brave girl, Ryan rewarded me with lunch at my favorite Greek restaurant in Nashville where I thoroughly enjoyed lemon rice and chicken meatballs, which, I can proudly say, I've now perfected as a dinner option at home.

Being vulnerable leads to tenderness. Tenderness leads to intimacy. I didn't want to confess my weakness to my husband, but had I withheld how I was feeling, I would have withheld a great gift he could have given me: the gift of his tenderness. Oh, and a week later I logged into the online portal and everything was fine and dandy, just like Ryan said it would be.

- 2 lbs ground chicken
- Salt and pepper to taste
- 2 Tbsp milk
- 2 Tbsp parsley
- Olive oil

Place ground chicken in a large bowl. Add milk, salt and pepper, and parsley. Form into small balls. Coat a skillet with olive oil and cook the meatballs on medium heat until no longer pink. Remove from pan. Serve with your favorite rice and sauce.

Don't Look in the Rearview Mirror

You want to know something a bit strange about your friend Jess? Since my marriage to Jason, I have lived in nine homes, and after moving, I have never gone back to any of them. Like never, ever. Never even drove by the property to reminisce or see what the new owners have done to spruce up the place. When I leave a home, I am gone for good. It's part of my refusal to wallow in the past. Yes, the past shapes us, and we should respect the lessons it brings to our lives, but I don't see how seeking out pain by repeatedly returning to something, especially something that was left behind either by choice or force, can lead to anything positive. I see friends seemingly looking to the past on social media; happily married men and woman searching for former boyfriends or girlfriends and then sending them friend requests. *Why?* I wonder. It feels a bit dangerous, playing with fire, particularly if you had a romantic or sexual relationship with the person, similar to what Lot's wife did when she was commanded to run and not look back. That didn't end so well for her, did it?

> But Lot's wife looked back, and she became a pillar of salt. (Gen. 19:26)

The year Jason died was the year Facebook really began to gain momentum. Social media offered this new fun adventure for everyone! Who doesn't wonder from time to time what happened to a long-lost love or the friend who moved away when you were in fifth grade never to be seen again? I wondered many of these things, and as my husband lay silent in the den, exhausted from yet another round of treatments, and as any lingering form of intimacy slowly eroded as his physical health waned, I found myself occasionally meandering down the rabbit hole Facebook offered. Sure, why not check out Tom from college and see what he's been up to? Or wow, Kate sure aged a bit since I saw her ten years ago. Or gosh, I should have held onto Brad when I had him! Look at him now! A millionaire; what a life I could have had! We are all guilty of the comparison game, and social media has amped up the pressure a million times over; but is it really the best way to spend our precious time playing the "what if" game?

As Jason slept silently on the hospital cot behind me, I did connect with a few of these individuals whom I once had known. Grief will make you do crazy things, and honestly, the "what if" game was a way for me to check out of my grief. Nothing inappropriate happened, but I did find myself lamenting over a handful of

former flings—almost wondering if I still had "it," whatever appeal
I once had. If Jason died, would any man find a young widow with
four children appealing? Would I have any chance of having skin
in the game? I'm always one to have a back-up plan for a back-up
plan, and this was my strange and weird way of trying to control a
situation in which I had zero control. My husband was in hospice,
and there was nothing I could do about it. Needless to say, some
of these men I connected with continued to reach out after Jason's
death, and then one day, a message popped up on my phone after
my remarriage to Ryan. Apparently, I still had something.

"Hey Jess!" he hollered across the room. "You got a message
from some guy named Dave. By the way, who's Dave?"

"Oh, some guy I dated in college," I nonchalantly replied.

"Was it serious?"

"Eh, you know. I didn't date anyone for very long."

"Why is he sending you messages?"

"We reconnected on Facebook a few months ago, and every
now and then he checks in to ask how I'm doing."

"Hmmm," he replied, contemplating his desire that I not engage
with Dave and his desire to pursue peace—such a conundrum.

A thick, mysterious silence hung in the air as we both considered our next words.

"Honey, it's nothing really. I love you," I reassuringly said. "And
I get it. I wouldn't be comfortable with your ex-girlfriends texting
you, so I'll just shut it down."

It wasn't a big deal as we both aired our feelings about the situation. I knew it was playing with fire to have a close relationship
with the opposite sex, especially a relationship with someone I
was once intimate with. I had no desire to cause my new husband
any insecurities, and I vowed to be more careful moving forward
in our relationship.

I want to reiterate that I don't believe in playing with fire, but the insecurities that come with a brand-new relationship—like mine and Ryan's—do dissipate with time. Further down the road, it probably wouldn't have even hit his radar if some guy sent me a text; however, seeing that our relationship was new and hadn't had time to deepen and solidify, when Dave's text popped up on my phone, it did cause feelings of jealousy that I was happy to avoid. Just as I had been happy to leave my former homes in the past, I was happy to leave my former boyfriends in my rearview mirror in order for peace to reside in my new relationship.

Restoration

"I'm not doing this with you anymore!" I screamed at Ryan, grabbed my pillow and favorite blanket, and headed outside to the travel trailer. It was the same fight, and I was so sick and tired of going down this road. It came down to expectations in our marriage, and his expectation that women do women jobs and men do men jobs—except it seemed like there were a whole heck of a lot more woman jobs to accomplish with a family of ten than man jobs, which included weekly lawn mowing, scheduling oil changes, and fixing the occasional toilet leak.

We both worked full time, raised eight children, and prioritized our marriage, so it didn't seem fair that all the household chores plus the meals, laundry, dishes, filling out school forms, and making appointments, and, and, and . . . all fell on me because of a misogynistic idea Ryan had gleaned from childhood that "women do women jobs and men do men jobs." Yes, I enjoyed cooking, and no, I probably would not enjoy mowing the lawn or fixing the toilet, but enough was enough. The load I daily carried caused anxiety, stress, and overwhelm, and when I brought up to my husband how it would be helpful if he could lend a hand with dishes or laundry, his reply was, "I have a lot on my plate too, you know." Yes, I did know! We were both overextended by miles. I knew! But as I was crying out for help; I thought there would be a more empathetic response than, "I have a lot on my plate too, you know."

That last comment set off a barrage of ugliness; one accusation after another: "You never . . ." And, "I can't believe you said that!" And, "This conversation is literally making me sick!" And then the nail in the coffin: "I'm not doing this with you anymore!" I yelled as I stormed out of the house. I needed time to cool off, and I also knew that walking away from Ryan would greatly disturb his weary soul, and in that particular moment, I was out for a little disturbance. I was out for revenge, if I'm being entirely truthful.

Ryan has rejection issues. I knew this, and I knew my actions would hurt, and yes, I shamefully admit, that's what I was after. "An eye for an eye," as the good book declares. In this particular circumstance, I wasn't interested in the grace or mercy aspect that the good book also talks about. Right then, I wanted to cause him pain, and that's exactly what I did as I slammed the door extra hard and stormed off to our travel trailer.

Ryan's Take

I do have a more traditional approach to marriage but only by default. I grew up with a single mom who was forced to do everything around the house, and my sister and I had a daily chore or two to help out. "Men's work" and "women's work" were built into my subconscious through the years, and without having the hard conversations with my wife, they would still be there. I definitely made assumptions that Jess would take care of the kids and the house, and I would fill in the gaps when needed. In today's world, at least ours, if I expected her to take care of those things, she wouldn't have time for anything else. I have very little problem helping out with dishes or laundry or even cooking occasionally; but this particular day, I felt attacked, and it wasn't the subject matter that offended me. I had been struggling for months with physical pain and kept putting my head down and sucking it up until I could somehow make time for a much-needed surgery. That fateful day, I had been hanging drywall by myself and was physically miserable, which didn't help with my mindset when I walked in the door. When Jess implied I wasn't pulling my weight, it was the straw that broke the camel's back. I was pissed! And it takes a lot to get me fired up. Deep down, I knew her workload was much more demanding than mine, but anger has a tendency to mask that hidden wisdom in the heat of the moment. I can't remember anything about the argument that night, but I can remember the raw emotion both of us unveiled in a not so graceful way. We lashed out at each other, and a lot of unfortunate words lingered in the air long after she stepped away. It was painful. It was heartbreaking. And in the end, it was necessary. I won't pretend like we handled it well, but it took a true blowout to release the tension that had been building in both of us for years. When Jess walked out our back door with her blankets and pillows, I was ready to punch holes in the walls. I wanted to scream. I knew I had to calm down, and the separation helped.

I processed what had just happened, and when I stopped dwelling on what she had done wrong, I took a look inside. I wasn't pulling my weight, and I knew it. It wasn't intentional, but I was miserable and when I finally walked in the door at the end of the day, I was done, depleted. I had to dig deep to realize that reality wasn't anybody's fault but my own. My job was important, but my family was more important. Jess had too much on her plate, and as her husband and "helpmate," it was my job to recognize her need and change accordingly. Not an easy task but a necessary one. When I eventually calmed down, I made that tumultuous journey out the back door and gently knocked on the travel trailer door. After a little coaxing and a short conversation, she stepped out, and we headed to the kid's trampoline. We talked awhile, both mentally exhausted and ashamed of how horribly we had handled our latest squabble. We apologized and laid back on the springy tarp and stared at the stars hand in hand. At that moment, no words were necessary. We knew we had gone too far, and it was time to be quiet and let God do his work.

What merry-go-round do you need to jump off? What issue keeps popping up over and over again and makes you so angry, primarily because you're feeling like you're not being heard? It could simply be tied to exhaustion like ours was, or it might be something deeper, but you'll never know unless you get to the heart of the matter. Make time to pray about whatever it might be and then commit to having the hard conversations that will move you into a place of deeper intimacy and restoration.

NOTES

[1] *Collins English Dictionary*, Dictionary.com, s.v. "intimacy," accessed May 24, 2022, https://www.dictionary.com/browse/intimacy.

[2] Edward Mote, "My Hope Is Built on Nothing Less," *1017 Hymnals* (1834).

SEX

Some Want More than Others—Why It's Important

As I sat down to write this chapter, my mind went blank and my heart started to race, and I sent my friend a text.

"I'm writing the chapter on sex, and I don't know how to talk about this!" I wailed with lots of crying emojis.

Her response: "You'll do great, Jess."

Here goes . . .

Last year, I was down with COVID, and I binged a show called *Married at First Sight*. The premise is pretty self-explanatory. Two strangers meet at the altar and get married. Most of the marriages end in divorce. As I watched, one contestant said something that irritated me. His friend asked how his marriage was going, and he offered a glowing report about his new wife. He gushed about her beauty, drive, and personality; however, when asked if he would

83

stay married, he faltered. Why? Because they hadn't had sex yet, and he wasn't sure he could marry someone without knowing how the sex would be. He asked, "What if we're not compatible?"

"Try it before you buy it" is a popular viewpoint, and if it's not the most amazing experience ever, then you must not be compatible, right? What a sad way to view an intimate experience with your spouse. Sex should be a big deal in marriage, but if you love someone and are committed, isn't this an area you could grow in? Get better at fulfilling one another's needs over time? The Lord made sex as a gift that only a spouse is supposed to fulfill: "rejoice in the wife of your youth, a lovely deer, a graceful doe. Let her breasts fill you at all times with delight; be intoxicated always in her love" (Prov. 5:18–19 ESV).

I'm not sure about Ryan viewing me as a lovely doe, but let's examine this admonition to stay faithful—and not only faithful but intoxicated faithfulness! First comes commitment (rejoice in your spouse) and then intimacy follows (let her breasts fill you with delight). There have absolutely been days when I have not rejoiced over my husband. If I start the day off in a petty, grumpy manner, Ryan will follow my lead, and before we know it, we're throwing daggers at each other. But, if I shift my mindset to thankfulness, this sets us up for a different outcome, which might include intoxicated intimacy! But why is sex important in marriage, and if it's not currently important, why not? I understand, life is busy or there might be health problems to consider—I'm familiar with this road—but if we're healthy and living somewhat normal lives and still not regularly connecting sexually with our spouse, we should explore *what's preventing intimacy?*

Also, how much sex is enough? One partner may have a high sex drive and the other may be satisfied with once a month. Where's the happy medium, and how do we arrive at a place where each feels respected and heard in this delicate area? Is "enough" a word we should use in discussions about sex? Enough can imply that one person wants something and the other will oblige but not willingly. I have an acquaintance who believes her husband's sexual pleasure is not her problem. I would contend that this philosophy will probably lead to resentment and issues down the road and is not a theory based in Scripture: "Do not deprive one another, except perhaps by agreement for a limited time, that you may devote yourselves to prayer; but then come together again, so that Satan may not tempt you because of your lack of self-control" (1 Cor. 7:5 ESV). When the Bible makes a bold "Do not" statement, it is in our best interest to obey.

Let's begin by looking at desire, the cornerstone of sexuality. Once this is addressed, we can add concerns like spice, the consequences of sexual sin, and practical ways to move forward, step-by-step, in the direction of a satisfying sex life for both partners so that it doesn't become a chore or an obligation.

Y'all ready for this?

Here goes!

Desire Starts with You

"Do I ever turn your head anymore?" I asked him, slightly nervous about the answer I might receive. I slowly leaned away as we sat facing one another on the sofa, bracing for the rejection I was sure to hear. There's that blunt personality trait again. If I think there might be a problem, I address it; and lately, I didn't seem to interest my husband. This realization made me sad and anxious with ridiculous reasons such as, *He's not happy with the weight I gained*, or *my nagging has finally pushed him to a breaking point*, or *he wishes I would stop wearing leggings and T-shirts every day.*

You know, totally rational thoughts that women dwell on.

"What are you talking about?" he asked, looking up from the *National Geographic* magazine he was reading.

Granted, I sprang this question on him after I arrived home from a grocery store run with my two beautiful teenage daughters. It was during this excursion that my forty-four-year-old self realized the young college guys hanging out on the sidewalk did not whip their heads around for me as they once would have; but they did, instead, whip their heads all the way around for my teenage daughters. In a pathetic, middle-aged way, this made me sad. Yes, beauty is in the eye of the beholder, but it's a splash of cold water in the face (actually it's more like a full-body dunk into an ice-cold bath) when a middle-aged woman realizes she's no longer "got it." In other words, I no longer possessed the young, taut, outward beauty I once did, and now, due to perimenopausal hormones that did not know how to behave, I really wouldn't mind an ice-cold bath (maybe drawn by one of those hunky guys).

Just saying . . .

Now you have the back story for this random question I posed to my unprepared husband, and now he had to answer for my insecurities because I no longer had nineteen-year-old men checking me out. Lucky guy, huh?

"Yes, I still check you out." He smiled. "But there's a level of comfort that we now have. I'd take that any day over the raging hormones of when we were first dating; but of course, when you put on that cute blue dress, and we go out dancing in Mexico, I'm thinking, *dang, my wife is hot.* And yes, other men check you out too! Just not nineteen-year-olds," he joked with a wink.

I rolled my eyes.

"Okay," I smirked. "You know how I can get."

"Yes, I'm aware." He smiled, eyes diverted back to reading his magazine as I headed to the bedroom to relax. I puffed the pillows and situated a favorite throw across my lap as I got comfortable in bed. I landed on Netflix and found exactly what I was looking for. A show, or more accurately, a "chick flick," about an American girl who travels to Paris for a job. She's a true-blooded American obsessed with striving and working—as many of us are in the good ol' USA; however, in Paris, she meets Parisian women who teach her a different way of life. Their motto is *a life without pleasure is no life at all*. As I watched, I noticed a bigger lesson at play. I saw this high-strung American girl begin to enjoy pleasure and self-care. By desiring herself, she became desirable to most of the men she met, which led to an epiphany. I needed to desire me and choose pleasure, and then my confidence would affect other aspects of life—including my marriage—and I wouldn't have to beg my husband to turn his head or be down in the dumps when hunky college guys didn't look at me. I continued to watch and noticed a trend. The more pleasure the American allowed herself, the more desirable she became to everyone around her.

I decided that this chick was definitely onto something special. The show ended, and I immediately grabbed the phone to find the nearest salon and booked myself a pedicure, something I really enjoyed—like once a year—but why wouldn't I allow myself this pleasurable indulgence a little more often? What held me back? Money or time? I worked through these excuses, and it wasn't either. No, it had to do with this martyr mentality that many women possess and hold on to for dear life. It's ingrained in us to forego pleasure, especially pleasure for ourselves, but in doing so, we forego so much of what it means to be human, especially a woman! We are human beings, not human doings, so why don't we take more time to simply be? To be present? To enjoy little gifts here in life that put a smile on our face?

I vowed then and there to prioritize myself and, in turn, prioritize pleasure because Parisians are right: What is a life without these indulgences? And to really show how committed I was to the new-and-improved version of me who loves pleasure, I made the family crème brûlée for dessert. *Why not?* I reasoned. It's one of my favorites and a convenient way to use the surplus of eggs our chickens produce.

What brings you pleasure and how can you make these small indulgences a consistent priority in your life? Scented candles? Magazines? Pedicures, like me? Invest in yourself, and you might find that the joy you receive will pay numerous dividends in your relationships.

Crème Brûlée

- 5 Tbsp white sugar
- 1 cup heavy cream
- 3 egg yolks
- 1/4 tsp vanilla extract (or maple for a twist)

Preheat the oven to 350° F. Whisk 3 Tbsp sugar and heavy cream in a medium pot over low heat on the stove until combined. Remove from heat and whisk in eggs yolks and vanilla extract until smooth. Pour mixture into two ramekins and set these on a roasting pan. Pour in enough hot water into the pan to reach halfway up the sides of the ramekins. Bake about 50 minutes and then chill in the refrigerator for 2 hours. Remove and sprinkle 1 Tbsp of sugar on top of each. Broil in the oven for 30–60 seconds, until the tops are brown and bubbly.

Desire Me Too

"I'm often hurt because it seems like you would be fine without me. Like you don't really need me to run this ship."

Ryan, my passive peacemaker, oftentimes noncommunicative husband recently said this to me.

I was brainstorming about meals and schedules for the upcoming week and not terribly excited about being interrupted with this random thought, especially since the kids were about to arrive home from school and impede any progress I hoped to achieve. Ryan was prepping for another week out of town, and I was feeling bogged down and a bit crabby because I was about to be a single mom again, and I didn't understand where he was coming from.

"What do you mean?" I questioned, getting a bit defensive. "Of course, I need you. I'm not excited about doing life without you next week, but I am in full preparation mode so that it goes smoothly."

"I don't know." He sighed. "Sometimes it seems like I'm not needed, and you would be fine on your own because you're a strong woman. You don't need a man."

I replied, "I would survive if I had to. I was on my own after Jason died and, yes, I managed but it wasn't my choice to be alone. I want you in my life but, no, I probably don't need you for survival. Need implies entrapment. Want implies a choice. But honey," I continued, "I do require you for all the things that need fixing. If I didn't have you, I would have to hire hunky guys to help out." I winked, hoping to diffuse the tension. "I chose to have you in my life. I made vows to you, and personally, I would rather be chosen than feel like an obligation that had to be fulfilled."

We both sat there, silent for a moment.

"I'll have to think about that," Ryan quietly responded. "Just so you know, as a man, it's nice to be needed by your wife."

"And I'll think about that," I replied with a grin. "But to reassure you right now, I do enjoy having you beside me and would not want to do this life without you. In fact, while you're gone the next couple of days, I won't sleep well because there's this foreboding feeling that everything falls on me. I appreciate the sense of calm you bring to my life; so yes, I do need you in order to sleep well—just beside me, in a different bed."

We both laughed.

"But now," I suggested with a smirk, "why don't we have a little fun before the kids arrive home, and I can show you how needed you are."

That comment obliterated any remaining tension as we hurried off to the bedroom and quickly locked the door.

I understood his insecurities as I often felt the same; but in hindsight, what we were trying to convey in our human weakness is that there is a hole in our spirits that neither one of us or any other person could possibly fill. I love having Ryan in my life, but he can't fill me with a peace that passes understanding no matter how hard he tries. He can lock every door before bed and sleep with a bat under his mattress, but our true help and salvation are from the one we had both surrendered to years ago, our Savior, who was the only one who could truly provide the all-abiding reassurance we needed, including the peace I desperately craved after a tragic memory unexpectedly resurfaced in my marriage.

Sexual Graveyards

Deep breath.

A few years into my marriage with Ryan, I was going about my day, doing dishes, making food—you know, the things moms typically do. I started a bath for Josh and Jada, ran down to take dinner out of the oven and back upstairs to check on them, and then I stopped dead in my tracks at the top of the staircase. I stood silent and still as the images flooded over me. The smoky haze, the door being held shut against my will, the genitals in my face. I hadn't thought about these memories in years; memories tucked deeply into an untapped crevice in my mind. I fell to the floor and covered my face with shaking hands and wept with the realization that I had somehow forgotten about these moments that had occurred years ago when I was attending college.

I was sexually assaulted and never told anyone because I didn't think I would have been believed.

Twenty plus years ago, I was a nobody, and my assailants were somebodies, athletes to be specific, untouchable athletes who attended a Christian college. They were under the influence. I was not. I didn't even know what being under the influence looked like and only figured it out years later as I connected the dots, the smells, the laughter, and the heavy eyelids. Back then, I was a naive, homeschooled girl way out of her league and flattered by the attention. I was sexually assaulted, and it was wrong. They committed a horrific act against me that will never be erased from my life.

I went there alone, that fateful afternoon, as a naive nineteen-year-old. I entered the apartment of a man I knew, an athletic star, a man I was casually seeing—a man who was casually seeing quite a few women unbeknownst to me at the time. I'll call this man Bob. I assumed I would eventually win Bob's heart through my desperate devotion and desire. He knew how much I adored him and preyed on that knowledge. He became my teacher as I clumsily navigated my way through a new and unfamiliar environment, an environment so completely different than the innocent, sheltered, homeschooled life I had experienced.

I knocked on his door, and he opened it. A cloud of hazy smoke welcomed my arrival; at the time, I assumed the joint in his hand was a cigar—yes, I was very naive. Through the haze, I noticed two large men, teenage men, sitting on a battered couch with a coffee table littered with empty beer cans in front of them. These were also star athletes from a few towns away.

The details leading up to the incident are fuzzy, maybe due to fear or perhaps the protective nature the brain offers, but I remember being summoned into the bedroom by Bob, who smirked as he suggested I could help him study for an upcoming test. We sat on the bed together, and the two other men immediately joined us.

I was confused. Bob quickly rose, left the room, and slammed the door shut—leaving me alone with the two men I had just met. Two huge men towered over me while Bob tightly held the door shut. I heard hysterical laughter coming from him, and so I assumed it was a joke. A very bad joke.

I waited for the joke to be over, but it didn't seem to be headed in that direction. The two men sat beside me and formed a tight barrier that made escape difficult. They also seemed to find the situation highly entertaining as they laughed and began discussing random sexual activities along with their presumptions that I probably lacked experience. They suggested that I should be tested to see if I knew what I was doing in the areas of sexuality, and if not, it would be a good idea for them to teach me. I nervously laughed and said probably not—still trying to be cool about the uncomfortable situation I was in. I didn't want to get a reputation as one of those girls who was dramatic and couldn't take a joke. My denial, sadly, was not in being horrified that two men thought they could joke about using me as a sexual pawn but had more to do with how Bob would react if he knew what was going on behind the closed door. At the time, I wasn't willing to risk losing the precious, nonexistent relationship I had with him.

I tried to stand, and one of them grabbed my hair and shoved me back onto the bed. What happened next horrified and humiliated me. Memories that haunt me as I write this. Tears streamed down my face, and I begged them to stop as laughter loudly resounded from the other side of the door.

I know it ended somehow, but past those horrific moments, I have no recollection. I don't know why I can't think past the point of being held against my will. At times, I fear that I've blocked out something too terrible to recall, and at times, I pray that's as far as the assault went. I don't know how I finally left the room. I don't know if I sat and talked with the three of them after it was finished. I don't know if they continued laughing. I assume they did. I do know I didn't blame Bob for what occurred. Somehow my mind was able to separate him from them for years until I just couldn't anymore.

Back then, I didn't know I had rights. Rights for what? I put myself in the situation. I chose to associate with Bob, which in turn meant I associated with his acquaintances. I didn't even know what an experience like that would be called. I didn't know if it was partly my fault because I had gone over there alone. I did know it would be my word against three athletes—three athletes who all started on their respective teams.

I used to think that's just how men were, and it was a woman's responsibility to accept it—"boys will be boys."

I can say with confidence that if something similar happened today, I would die before allowing anyone to desecrate me the way they did. I also know that I've forgiven them even though they've never asked, and I am grateful that now the law more frequently serves justice toward men who have the audacity to think they can treat women in such a horrific, uncaring way. This fact alone will enable my daughters to have a different college experience than I had. They will not be afraid to come forward, God willing.

This incident had the potential to really wreak havoc on my marriage, but Ryan is one of the good guys. When he found me at the top of the stairs, hyperventilating as I relived the experience, he wept and entered into the pain with me, and I was able to begin to heal. He didn't blame me. He blamed them. He wasn't angry with me. He was angry at them. He would have protected me, and I saw that in his deep despair. He held me and whispered words of comfort and gave me a gift. He gave me space to heal and never once suggested that the outcome could have been different. He never suggested shame, and it was in that moment that I was able to move toward forgiveness.

Had Ryan reacted differently, our story today might be different. I would have distanced myself from him if he had not provided a safe space for my grief. He gave me a gift in his reaction of love and comfort rather than of judgment.

Consider your past. What needs healing for movement forward into the beautiful fullness of sexuality with your spouse? Past sexual partners? A pornography addiction? Rape? Incest? Own it. Speak it. Write it down and burn it if need be. You cannot heal from what you don't acknowledge, and this acknowledgement will be the first step in releasing spiritual bonds so you can experience true love and intimacy in your relationship—a lesson my husband would also have to face in his own sexual graveyard.

Ryan's Confession

Ryan here. I'm going to talk about a sensitive subject that most men don't want to face, especially in front of the whole world. We considered adding this chapter to Jess's last book, *Blended with Grit and Grace*, but I wasn't ready to share my transgressions. I had just about made up my mind to leave it out of this book too until I read the latest statistics about pornography, with 40 million Americans routinely viewing pornography and 64 percent of Christian men consuming it on a regular basis; and there were more gut-wrenching stats about women and children.[1] I was temporarily proud to be one of the less than 36 percent, which honestly, I bet is a much lower percentage, but it's difficult to get men to admit to this problem. I say temporarily because it wasn't always the case.

I was exposed to pornography at around six years old. I lived in a working-class neighborhood, which meant Mom and Dad both worked (or in my case just Mom), so the kids I grew up around had a lot of freedom. Basically, from the age of six, I had access to multiple inappropriate magazines, and before the age of ten, I had even watched XXX rated movies. I knew it was wrong, and the guilt of it hung on me like a weighted blanket I carried for many years. Porn became an outlet, a fantasy life only I was aware of, and it allowed me to avoid whatever bad thing was going on in my young life. It gave me, what seemed at the time, comfort—unhealthy, I realize, but comfort nevertheless. It deeply gripped my soul and subconsciously held on for many years.

I assumed it would be easy to let go of it once I was married because it seemed to be about sex. It turns out, it wasn't. A few times a year when life wasn't going the way I expected it to be, it would creep back. A short fantasy followed by overwhelming guilt and a new promise to myself and to God that it was the last time.

I've been asked, "Why wasn't it an issue during good times?" Pornography was a coping mechanism that started early in my childhood that would allow me to live in a fantasy world void of hardship and expectations. When life is good, the fantasy life is unnecessary. It's similar to drinking: having a glass of wine or a beer when celebrating an anniversary or an accomplishment is not a problem; but when times are bad, this celebratory act can become a coping mechanism, going too far for many with a bottle of wine or a six pack. Coping mechanisms can vary, but they typically serve the same purpose: a way to numb the pain. My bad habit would only show up when I needed to disappear. One of the worst things about it was it never made me feel better, it only added more guilt and deepened the crevice of pain and shame. But for some reason, the shame became my safety blanket that I cozied up inside whenever life became more than I could bear. While I was writing this, an early reader asked how porn affects the brain, and I thought I'd give a real-life illustration of how I approached that question.

Me: (speaking to Jess) I'm not an expert on the subject; I don't know how to answer.

Jess: (in her straightforward manner) Google it.

Me: I don't think it would be a good idea for me to google "how porn affects the brain."

Jess: Why not? I'm sure there are a million articles on the subject.

Me: There probably are, but I'm more concerned about what else will show up in the search.

I've had to accept the fact that I need accountability from here on out. There are a number of triggers that are out of my control, but I must tame those within my reach to avoid being overwhelmed.

When I married Jess, I thought porn was behind me, but with our new marriage came new challenges, many I didn't know how to fix. Porn became a demon I couldn't resist without outside help. When Jess discovered my hidden secret, it was devastating. I never understood why or how my problem could affect her, and so I kept it buried deep within my soul. A secret I would always keep to myself, thinking she didn't need to know. I didn't dare share something so vulnerable. It was an issue in my life that I couldn't beat, and it made me feel weak and exposed; and the guilt, oh the guilt! I was a Christian! I was supposed to be one of the good guys! The exception to the rule! But I was just like everybody else: a sinner in need of grace.

When the whole truth was exposed, which you'll read about next, I saw a brokenness in Jess that I hadn't seen before. I was scared, not just about how disappointed she was in me but that it could be the end of our relationship. That realization had never occurred to me before, but in that moment, I knew it was time. I met with therapists about it, and they would nonchalantly talk with me and remind me that I was human, and it wasn't my fault. That's bullshit. Sorry, but there's no other way to say it. It wasn't my fault when I was exposed as a child, but it became a choice when I became a man. As it says in 1 Corinthians 13:11 (ESV), "When I was a child, I spoke like a child, I thought like a child, I reasoned like a child. When I became a man, I gave up childish ways." And I wasn't being a man. At least not the man God created me to be. I had to take ownership, and I'm proud to say I did. I repented and eventually told Jess everything and have never looked back. I no longer have that demon in my life. It hasn't been an easy road, but the weight that has been lifted has changed me. It took admitting that it was sin, and that I had broken my marriage vows to Jess. It was hard to admit that I had committed adultery.

For any men reading this (the few of you), this has to be the first step in beating back this beast, because it's not something that will go away on its own. This can be our "Gladiator" moment, because this foe is one of the most powerful enemies our world has ever known, and we have to dig deep for the strength to overcome it. You need someone to hold you accountable no matter how awful it makes you feel. Jess and I read lots of books on the subject, and she has forgiven me; but it was much more difficult to forgive myself.

Here are a few tangible actions that have helped me in the fight against pornography.

- I gave Jess my phone and asked her to put a password on it restricting access to anything inappropriate. This is how serious I am about avoiding temptation.
- She also knows any passwords I have on devices, and she can grab my phone or computer and check it anytime she wants.
- The struggle has gotten easier as the years have passed, but to keep my guard up daily, I pray every morning for strength because I cannot do this on my own. I echo the sentiments of the apostle Paul in 2 Corinthians 12:9 (ESV): "'for my power is made perfect in weakness.' Therefore, I will boast all the more gladly of my weaknesses, so that the power of Christ may rest upon me."

The Day Everything Changed

Jess here.

I remember the day vividly: a typical day in January 2012, about nine months into my new marriage. Ryan and our daughters flew to Oklahoma to visit family while I stayed home with the boys, specifically with Lucas whom we rarely took on vacations because of his intense needs. I understood that Ryan craved time in his old stomping grounds, his hometown, and I gave my blessing even though I had an excessive amount of anxiety tied to his departure as his absence often caused an immediate transport back to the lonely days after Jason died. My feelings during this particular departure hinged on obsessive, and I was terrified I would never see him again.

The moment Ryan drove away, the anxiety and despair increased. My chest tightened as I relived those lonely months after I became a widow, and I began to obsess about an issue I had repeatedly inquired about with Ryan but never fully believed the answer I was given, which was a version of, "Babe, you're over-thinking. There's nothing I'm hiding. I promise."

But that's not how it felt; however, I always caved and dismissed any concerns as grief or insecurity. We openly discussed topics that would have been avoided with Jason and Kaci—specifically the topic of intimacy and what our expectations were in our relationship. We also discussed my expectation for sexual purity, a topic close to my heart after a friend's husband had recently admitted to a lifelong pornography addiction, which led him into the arms of another woman.

As this lonely night progressed, the feelings grew intense, and I searched for something to journal in, a habit that had helped clear my mind in the past. I found a pile of blank notebooks I had inherited from Ryan's previous life perched high on a kitchen shelf, so I grabbed one and then lounged comfortably in our bed. I began thumbing through the stark, white pages, and stopped. One page wasn't blank and was instead filled with words from the grave. Kaci, Ryan's first wife, journaled with a concerned heart about a confession from Ryan admitting his struggle with pornography. I sat there staring at the words, my suspicions having just been confirmed. I immediately called him, angry words spilling out as tears ran down my face: "I found something Kaci wrote," I began. "A confession about how you struggled with pornography."

He became defensive. "Why are you snooping?" he questioned.

I explained, "I opened one of the notebooks you gave me and found Kaci pouring out her heart."

Neither of us wanted to address the sensitive issue over the phone, and Ryan pacified me by explaining how Kaci had interpreted his admission of watching R-rated movies on business trips as a confession to watching pornography.

In my heart, I knew I wasn't getting the whole truth, but I didn't have any concrete evidence on which to base my accusations. He told me to rip out the journal entry, throw it away, and not worry about it again. Unfortunately, that was not the end of the story.

He arrived home later that week and continued to reassure me that what I found was nothing to worry about; but something was off. I knew it, and he knew it.

A month later, I discovered the truth.

He drove away for work one morning, and left alone, my suspicions crept in once again. The nagging thought that he was hiding something would not subside. There was his laptop—wide open. He had repeatedly said, "Look at it anytime. I don't have anything to hide."

But I wasn't so sure.

I took him up on the offer that day and searched his history. Initially, I didn't see any cause for concern, and his offer to "look anytime" was banking on my lack of tech skills. He didn't know me well enough at this point to also understand that I have an incredible drive for the truth and impeccable research skills. Google taught me everything I needed to know about computer cookies that day. I sat shell shocked as I stared blankly at the list of websites I saw before me, found deep within the belly of the hard drive. I printed off the list, wrote at the top "what I found on your laptop today," and placed it on the kitchen counter for him to contemplate when he arrived home.

The discovery that day led to more partial truths, and we wouldn't experience a complete uprooting of porn from our lives until after our move to Tennessee when a total brokenness occurred after the loss of our baby.

It took a year for us to get pregnant again after the miscarriage, and during that period, Ryan broke every last chain of lust and pornography in his life and within our marriage. God used that fallow year to grow something deeper in both of us. He used that year of despair and questions to free Ryan from the bondage of sexual sin and to free me from distrust and thoughts of retaliation. A month after he experienced true peace and freedom, we saw two pink lines show up on a pregnancy test. Nine months later, our beautiful baby girl Annabelle was born, our blessing through faithful obedience.

Maybe you're a wife in a similar situation. Maybe you know your husband is struggling but don't know how to approach the conversation. Maybe you don't know but you wonder. Maybe your husband has admitted a struggle, and you don't know how to move forward in grace and learn to trust again. I can honestly say, eight years after this incident, that I do trust Ryan. I don't see any reason for concern now, but it took time to arrive at this place.

Here are a few helpful suggestions for the wives who find themselves in a similar battle in their marriages:

- It took me admitting that I am not perfect and in as much need of a Savior as Ryan before true forgiveness could occur. It was easy to point my finger at him, at his sin; and until I took a deep dive into my issues and my problems, I remained so focused on his sin that I was unable to offer grace. Once I accepted my sinful nature, I could then extend grace to him.
- I asked for way too many details. Don't do this. These details will haunt you. Be okay with vague admissions.
- Find a therapist or a close trusted friend to pray with you, cry with you, and mourn with you. Yes, there was a mourning period for me as I began to accept the reality that my husband did, in a sense, cheat on me with other women. Fantasies but still sexual unfaithfulness.
- And with that mourning, came the stages of grief (denial, bargaining, depression, anger, and acceptance). Denial, in the beginning: "He wouldn't, would he? He's a Christian!"

Bargaining: "I'm sure it was only an occasional thing," or "He told me he only thought about me while he watched." Depression: "I'm not sexy enough for him," or "If I had offered more sex maybe he wouldn't have looked at porn." Anger: "Maybe we need to get divorced! He cheated on me!" And acceptance, where I am today: It happened. I've forgiven him, and we move forward in grace.

- I still check in on the temperature of our sex life: "You good, honey?" We pray together every morning, and you better believe it, if I thought something reentered our marriage in the form of sexual sin, I would address it immediately. Sin breeds in secrecy. Don't let sin fester for even a moment. If you suspect that something is going on, it probably is. Ignorance is not bliss; believe me.

- Finally, if you are in an abusive relationship, either emotionally, physically, or sexually, please seek professional help immediately.

Snapshots

"Bye honey!" I waved to my husband. We were smack dab in the middle of our move from Tennessee to Michigan, and he was headed out of town yet again to prep our land for a house build. His leaving had become a regular occurrence during the past year of upheaval with two flip houses in Tennessee—also out of town—and our land in Michigan. What had once been a traumatic experience when one of us had to leave—yes, we have battled a few codependency issues due to the deaths of our spouses—had become easier due to the repeated occurrences; but it was still not something I enjoyed. It was hard for him to finish houses and clear land by himself, and it was hard for me to be the sole caregiver of eight children back home; however, there was no way around the issue, and we did what we had to do and tried to maintain positive attitudes.

A few days into my stint as a single parent and after the kids had been fed, bathed, and tucked into bed, I was feeling a bit frisky and decided to send my out-of-town husband a picture. A somewhat risqué picture. I took a shower and then pulled the two lingerie options I owned out from the back of my dresser drawer. These two items had been purchased for my honeymoon and hadn't seen the light of day in quite some time. But on this particular night, I was going to set aside any insecurities I had about my aging body, don the black lacy option, and text my husband a picture, which I was absolutely sure would delight him to his very core. Right? What husband doesn't want to receive a racy picture from his wife? I was sure I would be in the running for wife of the year with this great idea. I shimmied my body into the contraption, snapped approximately one hundred very awkward pictures, sent the one that didn't show my face because that seemed really awkward, and then I waited. I watched a show on Netflix. And then another show, and still no response. *What is going on?* I wondered. I decided to FaceTime Ryan, thinking maybe the reception was bad where he was. I picked up my phone and called him. He immediately answered.

"Hey, babe," he gasped, exhausted from working nonstop over the past three days. "How is it back home?"

"We're good," I replied. "But hey, did you get the picture I sent?"

"Oh yeah, that was nice."

"Nice?" I questioned. "That seems like every man's dream! To have their wife send a racy photo. That took a lot of courage, you know."

"It was nice honey, but honestly, what do you want me to do with it right now? I'm knee deep in work, exhausted, and when a man sees a picture like that, he wants to act on it. You're not here for me to act on it, so no, I didn't dwell on how sexy you looked because that would lead me down a rabbit hole I don't want to go down."

"I don't understand," I said. "I thought I was doing something you'd appreciate."

"You were," Ryan reassured me. "And I'd love for you to do it again, but not when I can't see you because that's just torture!"

"Alright," I admitted. "I get it. It took a lot of courage for me to send that photo, and now I feel rejected. We should talk about this more later because I need to understand your point of view, and you need to understand how your reaction is making me feel."

Ryan's Take

I'm sure there are a few men out there wishing their wife were willing to do what Jess did. And don't get me wrong, I appreciated it, but there was something else at play. As you read previously, I have struggled with sexual purity my whole life, and to receive a racy picture of my wife when it would be days before I could see her again could potentially lead me down a path I don't want to traverse. I loved that she was willing to be vulnerable, but then what? I said exactly that, "What am I supposed to do now?" I have a sexy wife, and I love seeing her in lingerie, but . . . I was eight hours away when those provocative pics were sent, and I couldn't actually see her in person for a while. I loved the playfulness of it and the banter that followed, but I explained that next time she had an inkling to send me a sexy picture to make sure I was around to show my appreciation.

Obstacles to Sex

Let me paint the picture. We had recently moved to Michigan and were temporarily living in a double-wide with six children while we built our dream-accessible home. We knew we would be living in this situation for approximately nine months, and we were concerned about how intimacy was going to occur in tight quarters with super thin walls and limited space and six children, including two teenage girls who were well aware of what sex was. If I'm being honest, we avoided the act for a while because we were so exhausted from the move (physically and mentally), and we weren't sure how we were going to overcome the obstacles I mentioned. There's not a woman alive (I don't think) who can comfortably wrap her mind around sex knowing that her children are in the next room—especially children who have a clue about what's going on in Mom and Dad's bedroom! Needless to say, we were able to get creative (sleepovers at friend's houses are a blessing!), but it did require planning to keep the fires burning during this challenging time.

Obstacles to sex are a familiar problem for many marriages. Some road bumps that immediately come to mind include children (obviously) and even more so teenagers (who do have a clue), age, hormones, health issues, time constraints, pain, and exhaustion. What are our options when these issues arise and sex can't be as often as one or both of us desire it to be?

First, we had to accept that it would be different for a time, and this was difficult because I'm a fixer. I'm not such a great empathizer, but if there's a problem, I immediately set to work on research and implementation of solutions. This is a positive trait—most of the time—but it can be a stressful trait to have in a partner if the other spouse truly can't help whatever ailment is preventing a healthy sex life. Jason and I encountered this problem when he underwent treatments for cancer. The exhaustion and pure inability to accomplish anything outside of survival became unavoidable for many years. I didn't mind so much because I had my own exhaustion with four young children, special needs, and cancer, so neither of us pushed the issue for a consistent sex life. We accepted that it was what it was and were hopeful that when he was cancer free, we could return to normal. Unfortunately, normal never occurred, and Jason gained his eternal wings on August 24, 2010.

Ryan and I also encountered a similar scenario when he landed in the ER in 2017. He was a complete space cadet due to the demands of our life and was not in a good place. This resulted in a lack of intimacy, which led to feelings of rejection and PTSD for me because in my history; if a husband didn't want sex, that meant he was going to die. Logical or not, that's where my mind goes when I have an ill husband.

Other obstacles you might face include a difficult diagnosis with a spouse or being fearful of sex during a high-risk pregnancy or a deployment as many military families are familiar with. These are legitimate reasons for why sex might not occur regularly; however, we can't let these circumstances become the norm.

When I heard the news that my unborn baby had a stroke in utero, I was terrified of having sex. I was convinced intimacy would cause further harm to the baby, and Jason respected this fear of mine; however, after Lucas was born, I was no longer fearful that sex would harm the baby but was instead exhausted from the challenges associated with raising a newborn with extreme special needs. Jason gave me grace—for a while—but then we had "the talk," which was basically him saying, "I miss my wife and want to resume intimacy in our marriage," and we concocted a plan that suited us both. Fast forward to teenagers and lots of kids who have lots of questions, and it has become much more difficult in my current life!

Generally speaking, women seem to be more accepting of drought periods, and I believe this is partially the result of soaking up so much love and attention from the blessed offspring we spend our days catering to that we find we don't necessarily crave more touching from anyone, including our husbands! However, ladies, your husband needs this from you! He feels closest to you right after sex, and this is how he expresses his love for you. I know, it doesn't make much sense, but it is how God wired him. Don't take this gift from him by withholding your affection; and if you're going through a challenging time that makes sex nearly impossible, talk about it. Resentments fester in silence and then these resentments often lead to revenge or bad choices like affairs or pornography. Deal with the issue head on. Communicate with one another. Open your heart to truly hear what your spouse is saying, and then create a plan for intimacy and make it happen.

Spice Is Nice

I rolled out of bed, grabbed a cup of coffee, got Lucas ready for school and on the bus, headed back inside, grabbed a refill on my coffee, and sat down at my computer where I intended to get caught up on emails. I opened the first account and began to scroll through the numerous inquiries that had arrived during my inactivity. As my career has grown and as I've become a familiar face in the arena of advocacy and special needs, I occasionally receive offers from companies interested in a partnership.

One email caught my eye. I stopped and open it: "Hi Jess! We love your content and would love to have you partner with us in our latest marketing campaign! We provide women with empowerment tools, and we think you'd be the perfect ambassador."

Hmmm, looked interesting. I clicked on the link and blinked away my surprise as the screen filled with the image of a lovely young woman holding a banana like contraption. A large vibrator to be precise. I laughed. Really, this company thought Jess plus her mess of eight kids and a blended family and special needs would be the perfect face to market vibrators? Oh boy. I shared the news with Ryan, and we chuckled, but it did get me thinking about the lack of spice in our relationship during the past couple of years. Sure, there were weekly date nights and sex, but the passion, the spice, the *oo la la* was missing—the passion we once held in spades as was portrayed in the first gift I received from my husband.

For our one-month anniversary, Ryan surprised me with a book he had created that detailed how I was his knight in shining armor. Our first year together was full of passionate displays of affection with surprise dates, romantic rendezvous in unexpected places, and flowers sent almost monthly. When our first wedding anniversary rolled around, in full Jessica fashion, I surprised my new husband with an album full of photos from a boudoir shoot I had secretly scheduled. He seemed quite pleased.

But now, there hadn't been any experiences like these in years. Somehow, we had gotten ourselves into a rut, and somehow, we needed to get ourselves out of the rut and back into sexy land; and I had an idea.

Remember our travel trailer that usually sat vacant in our backyard? I transformed it one evening into a love nest. I spruced up the bed, put a nice bottle of wine in the fridge, and then found a dainty little number I had purchased for Mexico a few years back and prayed that it still fit as I shimmied it up and over my thighs. It did, thankfully. I put Mya in charge, wrote Ryan a note to meet me, and then headed to the trailer to await my prince charming who eventually did arrive, a bit off kilter (he's not really sure how to respond to surprises); but once he figured out the meaning of the evening, he was a happy participant.

Spice is nice and really doesn't have to be expensive or extravagant. Ladies, your man wants you naked. It is that simple. If you want to wine and dine yourself (which I am all about) before he unwraps "the gift," do it and then share with him how you would also like him to instigate some spicy moments together in the future, preferably without unexpected guests like the experience I'll share next.

Boundaries

"Mom, Dad, I don't feel so good."

The door to our boudoir creaked open, and Ryan and I abruptly stopped but not before yanking the sheet up to our eyeballs as we both laid silently in the dark, barely daring to breathe.

I cautiously peeked out at the six-year-old shadow standing quietly in the door frame as the light from the moon shone on her pale, sunken face.

"I don't feel so good," she whispered.

"Just a minute, sweetie. Head back to your bed, and I'll be there in a second." Then as she turned to walk away, I admonished: "Oh, and honey, can you shut the door, please!"

She reached out and gently closed the door, and Ryan leapt out of bed to turn the lock.

We looked at each other in dismay. That was too close for comfort—even if she had no idea what we had been up to!

I quickly scurried to the sick child's bedroom and proceeded to find a bucket, cool her head with a cloth, and tuck her back in for the night.

All was better by the next morning, but the close encounter led to a family discussion around the dinner table the following evening.

"So, kids," Dad began, "we want to remind everyone that it's best to always knock on someone's bedroom door before entering—even Mom and Dad's."

The guilty child looked up from her dinner plate and tried to explain herself, "I'm sorry Dad, but I wasn't feeling so good."

"Yes, honey, we understand," he continued, "but in the future, we just want everyone to be aware that it's best to knock first. You never know if someone might be getting dressed or want their privacy for whatever reason." He let that last comment hang in the air.

The kids nodded their heads in agreement and promised they would try to remember to knock first, and Ryan and I agreed to try to remember to always lock our door when extracurriculars were on the table.

The act of locking the door has actually been beneficial for a couple of reasons. One, we no longer have unwanted guests during certain activities, and two, it's a signal to the other that there's desire on the table. This has been helpful for me because there are times when I need to wrap my mind around what my husband wants. When he walks into the bedroom and locks the door, I *know* what he's after. And he knows that it will take me a little bit of time to unwind from the day and get into a head space where I'm receptive to his desire. Shockingly, eleven years into marriage, it's not like the movies where we hop into bed and passionately rip each other's clothes off. We had a good run with those endorphins but now the passion has cooled a bit. Honestly, I'm not always in the mood, but that disclosure to my husband sometimes opens the door for negotiations, and ladies, these requests have never been denied.

Bargains and Schedules

I knew he was in the mood, and I also knew I was tired and grumpy and not in the mood. My head was pounding from my bickering children, and I felt overwhelmed with an upcoming move and a looming book deadline. My husband occasionally gets this "come hither" look and then inches close, and I felt annoyed at the thought of having to fill another love tank before I could pass out from the day. I proceeded with blunt honesty: "Honey, I know you're in the mood, and I can get there too, but I'm really not there right now; so if you could rub my head for a few minutes and release some of the tension then I think I'll be in a better place in thirty minutes or so."

Surprisingly, he agreed.

Thirty minutes later I did feel better. My headache dissipated, and I was relaxed and able to not only endure what was coming but find enjoyment as well.

This wasn't the first time we have bargained to get what we want. It's not a tactic we consistently employ, but it is a valuable tool to have in a marriage. I don't feel like sex is just another chore if Ryan's also willing to sacrifice some of his time to meet a need of mine. This method has worked in other ways as well and is especially effective during stressful times when I yearn for intimate touch (back rub, head rub, foot rub) because this relieves my stress, and Ryan yearns for sex because that relieves his stress.

There have also been times when one or both of us was too busy or felt too overwhelmed to even think about sex. I can tend to get this way, especially when prepping for fundraisers or feeling pushed up against a deadline. It's hard to release the overwhelm and fully engage in intimacy when I feel like my to-do list is running away from me! It's not even that I have to accomplish everything on it, but I do feel the need to organize my thoughts, a brain dump as I like to call it, so that the thoughts leave and end up on paper where I won't forget. Then I can usually get in the mood. However, there have been occasions that we've both been so overwhelmed that we haven't thought about sex in quite some time, and this has led to resentments. This is when we've had to actually say to each other, "Look, do you realize it's been X number of days or weeks since we've had sex? This isn't good for our marriage, so when should we make a date?"

True story.

And then we look at our schedules and figure it out! It might be a morning quickie, it might be an evening delight, or it might look like a Sunday afternoon "nap!"

I laugh at this because growing up, my next-door neighbor's parents often took a "nap" on Sunday afternoons while she and I quietly played with our dolls in her bedroom. Ryan and I also enjoy Sunday afternoon naps, and yes, we often sleep because we're tired, but every once in a while, we tell the kids we're taking a nap, lock the door, put a movie on, and lean in closer to one another.

I'm not the only one who benefits from a bit of bribery. I've been known to make this specific apple pie for Ryan when I have a super special favor to ask him that might require a bit of heavy lifting, like laying a patio in our backyard or putting together the sauna that I ordered from Costco; those unavoidable household tasks that no one wants to accomplish!

A few pieces of Ryan's favorite apple pie with Grandma Holly's pie crust usually will do the trick.

Apple Pie with Grandma Holly's Easy Pie Crust

Pie Crust (makes 2)

- 2 sticks of chilled butter chopped in small pieces
- 2 1/4 cups all-purpose flour
- 2 pinches salt
- 2 tsp sugar
- A few Tbsp of ice water

Filling

- 6 or 7 apples (or to fill crust) cut into slices, skin on or off
- 1/2 cup maple syrup
- 1 tsp cinnamon

Topping

- 3/4 cup flour
- 1/3 cup butter
- 1 cup sugar

Start with the dough: Blend dry ingredients for the crust in a mixer with a paddle attachment. Add butter and blend for about a minute. Slowly add ice water, a teaspoon at a time. You do not want a wet dough! Wrap in plastic wrap and chill in the fridge for about an hour.

Remove dough from fridge and split in half. Roll out one half until it fits in a pie pan. Pinch edges to form a crust (save second crust or make another pie). Combine apple slices, maple syrup, and cinnamon in a bowl and stir. Spoon into pie crust. Combine topping ingredients and sprinkle over the apple mixture. Bake at 350° F for about an hour. Check the edges at around 45 minutes and place foil around them if they are looking too dark.

NOTE

[1] Michelle Habel, "How to Overcome Porn Addiction and Restore Relationships," Focus on the Family, January 7, 2019, https://www.focusonthefamily.com/marriage /how-to-overcome-porn-addiction-and-restore-relationships/; "Pornography Statistics," Covenant Eyes, accessed July 15, 2022, https://www.covenanteyes.com /pornstats/.

4

HOUSEHOLD TASKS

Nonnegotiable Tasks and Peaceful Compromise

It's inevitable. There are nonnegotiable chores and obligations in every marriage that must be accomplished on a regular basis for there to be a well-oiled machine. Some of these obligations have to do with children, some with hidden tasks or expectations within gender roles, and some have to do with the never-ending daily grind of who is going to wash the dishes. Not me, said the mom! Dishes and laundry are the absolute bane of my existence, but that doesn't mean these chores magically disappear. How do we delegate these duties? And does the delegation derive from preconceived ideas? If so, is there merit to these ideas brought to our marriages through our upbringings, cultural expectations, or even biblical teachings? Is it fair to hold these expectations in our twenty-first-century relationships, or should we reevaluate their importance in light of the current culture? Instead of assuming these expectations will be ordained in our marriage, we might have to have a healthy chat about what will work for our situation.

Some issues are worth the heated discussions, and some are not—and some, we simply must buck up and get 'er done. Only you and your spouse can decide what you can live with and what must be addressed in a respectful manner focused on teamwork and resolution. Maybe your final resolution looks like cutting back on extracurricular activities so there isn't as much on your plates. Maybe it looks like getting takeout once a week to have a break from making dinner. Or implementing a chore system so the kids can help out. Maybe you can't cut anything, and it's time to hire help! In my life, the "what's for dinner" question (and cleanup) was one issue that had to be addressed for my peace of mind, or fireworks were going to explode, and not the kind from the previous chapter.

Delegating Duties

It was a quiet Saturday afternoon, and the family was relaxing. I was in the bedroom enjoying a movie, Ryan was sprawled out on the couch watching football, and the kids were engaged in screen time. My movie ended, and I stretched out on the bed as the credits rolled on by. I hazily glanced over at the clock. What?! It was already 4:30! My relaxation time abruptly ended with the realization that I had no idea what the dinner plan was, and Lucas's internal dinner bell promptly rings at 5:00 before his hollering to "GO EAT!" begins to reverberate throughout the house. I reluctantly rose, put fuzzy slippers on my feet, and shuffled out into the family room, darting a glance toward my husband who hadn't moved in hours.

"Must be nice to be the dad in this household," I muttered under my breath.

I was ignored, which does not sit well in my soul.

I amped up the pressure a few notches: "I don't know why I have to cook the meals, clean up the mess, and do the dishes every day," I muttered as I walked past him, completely oblivious as to when, where, or how his food would magically appear later that evening.

"I'm not a mind reader!" he replied. "Ask for what you need, and I'm happy to help."

"I don't know why I have to ask you to help. It bothers me that you don't ask me to help you order groceries or prepare meals or clean up. No, if you do the dishes there's an expectation that I say thank you for doing the dishes. Why? No one thanks me for ordering groceries or cooking meals or cleaning toilets or filling out school paperwork or making dentist appointments or . . ."

"Let me stop you right there. I get the point." He stood to his feet. "Got it," he said, obviously irritated. "You don't have to thank me for helping anymore."

"It's not that," I said even more irritated that he wasn't hearing what I was trying to say.

Well, maybe it was.

"Why is there an expectation that I thank you for helping with everyday chores? No one thanks me for diddly squat! No one even notices that groceries and meals magically appear every day. In fact, I usually get grief because I didn't fill out this particular paper on time or make this appointment or why are we having this disgusting dinner again. I'm sick of being the punching bag in the family!"

And with that I slammed down the wooden spoon I had been using to stir leftovers, which I was sure would elicit more moans and groans from the peanut gallery later that evening.

Casserole again! Why are there so many vegetables in it? Mom! Why can't you just make hotdogs like normal moms?

Such a good time being a mom. I needed a break.

I turned to my husband, "I'm going to our bedroom to stretch for a few minutes before dinner, okay?"

"Sure," he replied. "What do you want help with in the meantime?"

"Please just keep stirring the leftovers," I requested.

I retreated to decompress and took a few big breathes before reemerging to greet my family at the dinner table. Something had to give. It was time to have a conversation about expectations.

We ate dinner in silence, and everyone helped clean the mess because there was a thick feeling of "mom is not happy" still hanging in the air. Later that night, Ryan and I discussed our expectations for the numerous chores involved in our life. We both had a lot on our plates, and we had to simplify. Ryan's expectation was that women do "women's jobs" like laundry, cooking, cleaning, school papers, and appointments, but the problem was that with our situation, there were a lot of jobs for the woman to do, and I was feeling overwhelmed and underappreciated. He had received this perception of male and female roles through his childhood experiences where his mom basically took care of everything as a single parent, but—she only had two children. That system wasn't going to work for me as a working parent with eight kids.

That night we hacked out a plan:

- Before getting angry, Jess will ask Ryan to help. He's happy to help but doesn't always see everything that needs to be accomplished like Jess does because she is the all-seeing, all-knowing Queen of this home. I made that part up.
- Kids will help clean up the dinner mess and also help with an after-school chore like folding laundry, scrubbing

toilets, or pulling weeds. Ideally, they will cheerfully sing "whistle while we work" while accomplishing these tasks.

- Once a week, Dad will be in charge of dinner, and Mom will be okay with whatever Dad makes.
- Before devotions, the entire family will participate in a fun ten-minute family clean-up time where we set a timer and bust out whatever we can for ten minutes.
- Jess will hire help where she feels stretched too thin.

One of Ryan's favorite meals to make on his meal night is chicken fried rice, and the kids (and even Mom) love it too! Here's his tried-and-true recipe.

Chicken Fried Rice

- 3 large chicken breasts
- 1 package (12 oz) of mixed frozen vegetables
- 2 cups rice
- Bone broth or water
- Salt and pepper
- 1 stick of butter (8 Tbsp)
- Soy sauce
- 3 large eggs, scrambled

Make the rice with the bone broth or water according to the directions. Put aside. Next, melt the butter in a skillet, add the chicken, salt and pepper both sides, and cook until the chicken is no longer pink. Remove and cut into small pieces. Do not clean the skillet! Add the eggs and scramble; add the rice, chicken, and vegetables. Add salt, pepper, and soy sauce to taste.

Help Please!

We don't splurge on much. Ryan and I are—for lack of a better word—cheap. We don't purchase name-brand clothes or fancy cars. Nor do we drop loads of money on date night, and we love a good bargain. We're the ones who walk into a store and don't even look at the new merchandise up front but instead saunter to the back racks, the racks with bright yellow signs signaling deep discounts. I know where the clearance shelves are in the local grocery stores—when I'm forced to go. But because we're cheap, we are also bad at prioritizing help for our life. We could probably use a housecleaner, a nanny, and a handyman, but because we are "I can do it" people, we tend to do too much. As our children have aged and now have their own ideas for managing their time, this mentality has changed. We've noticed our bodies aching more, and activities that were once easy now take a toll, making finding shortcuts for our busy lives a necessity.

One of those shortcuts has been grocery delivery, which is one of the greatest inventions of the twenty-first century. Seriously, I loathe grocery shopping. Aimlessly walking up and down aisles is not relaxing nor is loading the five hundred or so grocery bags into my van and then unloading them into the house and then, again, loading everything into the fridge/freezer/pantry.

I'm not talking about three or four bags. Nope, our average grocery store trip is probably around twenty to twenty-five bags, and then I'll forget something essential and have to run back out and do it all over again the following day. The bane of my existence . . . until Instacart! Hallelujah! No more mindlessly roaming the aisles of Walmart! No more loading bags into my van! No more unloading and attempting to get them into the house in one trip, and in the process yanking my back out of alignment because no woman should ever attempt to carry that much weight on her arms! No more quickly hiding the essential ingredients before someone decides to turn them into a midnight snack. No more.

The other area of our life that we've recognized a need for help in has been with Lucas. As he's aged, we've felt the toll that caring for him has taken on our mental and physical well-being. People often say, "I want to find help for my child with special needs, but I can't find it anywhere!" I have to say, I search for this precious commodity like my life depends on it because I truly believe it might. I use Facebook and Craigslist and word of mouth. I've interviewed at least ten people before settling on one good option. We've also hired our teenagers to help so that Ryan and I can prioritize date nights. It is difficult, but be persistent. Find the help you deserve. Don't give up. Your marriage and your family life might depend on it.

What can you incorporate today to make your life a little bit easier? It might be as simple as signing up for a grocery delivery service. Or hiring your children to help clean or fold the laundry. Your peace of mind is worth it. Your marriage is worth it. Just do it.

Diapers and Drudgery

I descended the stairs, immediately irritated by what was awaiting me with each scream originating from Lucas's bedroom. "Great, what a Good Friday this is," I muttered as the stench rose to greet my nose. Lucas required yet another diaper change, a chore that was becoming increasingly able to grate my very last nerve over the past few weeks as his father recovered from shoulder surgery—a recovery period that did not allow for diaper changes or Easter prep assistance. I had no idea how I was going to manage everything with a joyful heart, which was the much bigger issue at play, as we prepared to celebrate our Savior's resurrection.

I opened the door slightly and held my breath. The third of the day so far. My least favorite job in the whole world.

I did what was necessary, and as I prepared to leave, Lucas reached for my face, met my eyes, and sang in his sweet, jumbled way, "Oh God you are my God, and I will ever praise you."

He repeated the words until I agreed to join in with his child-like faith, which I did, slowly, and a little unwillingly because the smell still lingered in the air.

We sang together, over and over, which elicited a smile as big as the universe as he waved his head back and forth in rhythm to the music.

Oh God you are my God, and I will ever praise you.

I will ever praise you.

Ever? Always? Even in stinky, smelly, crappy times?

Praise you in everything, Lord?

Praise you as a stressed-out mom trying her best to hold this life together while her husband recuperates from surgery?

Praise you in changing my grown child's diaper? With no end in sight? Not even a potty-training goal?

Our family had experienced our fair share of crap over the past couple of years. We had endured Lucas's stretch in PICU, Ryan's surgery, a broken foot and health issues, numerous bouts of the flu, dissolved contracts, questions, concerns, what felt like a never-ending quarantine, and then a move.

Praise the Lord through it all? It's what I preach, right? Thankfulness in the tragedies of life? Choosing joy in the stank? Choosing to just keep livin'? In that moment, I felt like I could just about bottle up that cheery disposition and chuck it into the sea.

Lucas finished his song, and I knelt to put his socks and shoes on—me, an author, teacher, and nonprofit CEO, titles that bear no significance to him. What does matter is that I continue to meet his needs: changing diapers, feeding, and kneeling before him as I serve the least of these. Those who could not live without the gracious intervention of others.

Many years ago, a man named Jesus also knelt to serve, setting aside his titles: Messiah, God, and Creator. He washed dirty feet and associated with outcasts and then prostrated himself before humanity as the nails pierced his hands and his body lurched forward in agony. He humbled himself before the least of these: the leper, the whore, the crippled, the thief, and even you and me.

Jesus walked among the broken in body and in spirit; those who relied on the generosity of normal, everyday folks for their next breath; those who probably couldn't control their bladders or put shoes on without assistance. Jesus was found among the Lucases of the world doing what needed to be done; serving in whatever capacity their needs required—Jesus would have changed Lucas's diaper.

These daily moments I live: kneeling, serving, holding my breath; moments of holy annoyance that involve mundane work; holy like washing filthy feet; holy like hanging out with lepers; holy like being broken and bruised for all.

And on this Good Friday, a day drenched in uncertainty and fear for many, on this day and many others, as parents and caregivers, we walk the Via Dolorosa, "the way of grief," as the air is thick with hopeless despair, and the night is black and silent, and our souls are screaming in quiet desperation, *It is finished! We are finished!*

And yes, life as we know it is finished; it will never be the same.

But—

We hold on.

We hold on with every ounce of strength that remains within our weary souls because life is always intertwined with death. It is the way of the world. Sunday morning is around the bend, and the page will flip. The Lucases will leap for joy and the blind shall see!

Until then? We remember the holy mundane tasks—*this do in remembrance of me*—the bread and the wine, the body and blood spilled for us; and may this remembrance lead to an ongoing resurrection as we serve in uncomfortable spaces holding unpleasant smells, washing feet and changing diapers if need be, the reverent places of vulnerability and long silences often held in nursing homes, dingy hotel rooms, AA meetings, and special needs classrooms as we tend to the needs of others; the holiest of work as we care for the least of these.

A resurrected perspective.

A holy shift in attitude.

Greater love has no one than this: to lay down one's life for one's friends. (John 15:13)

When Expectations Clash

A few summers ago, Ryan and I had airline miles that we needed to use or lose, and we decided to go on a couple's trip, but we weren't sure where to go! I crowdsourced on Facebook, and after receiving numerous suggestions, we narrowed our options to Maine, Cuba, and New York City, each enticing in their unique ways.

We settled on New York City—a place we had both previously visited but neither had experienced as a married couple—and off we went!

The grandparents watched the kids, and we hired a caregiver to help with Lucas. My expectations were sky high. I viewed myself as a city girl at heart, and I couldn't wait to experience everything the Big Apple had to offer.

Ryan wasn't as enthralled about city life, but he was excited to get away with his wife without any obligations for the week.

We checked into our Brooklyn Airbnb and then scoured the local offerings for something fun to do.

I love all things Italian, and we spent our first day in Little Italy. Ryan educated himself on the subway, and we began our mile-long hike to the boarding station. We made our way toward Little Italy, where we thoroughly enjoyed pigging out on pasta and wine and topping off the evening with strawberry gelato. As the sun began to descend into the night sky, we decided to make our way back to Brooklyn.

We boarded what we thought was the correct train. It was not. We exited to what we thought was our neighborhood, but it was not. We exited into Brooklyn, but a vastly different landscape presented itself than the one we had left earlier that day. We exited to a strung-out man who tried to grab me while Ryan jerked me away from his reach. We exited to extreme homelessness. We exited to women of the night undressing my husband with their eyes as we aimlessly walked around trying to get our bearings.

"Honey," I hissed, trying to avert my eyes from the dark shadowy image that seemed to be following us, "I thought you knew where we were. Do you think we should stop at that gas station and ask someone?" I pointed across the street.

"I'm not going in there," he responded. "And yes, I thought I knew where we were too; but remember, I've never been here before! I'm doing the best I can!"

"Well, we're about to die if we don't figure out where we are or get back on the subway because I don't think we're in the right part of Brooklyn."

"You know," Ryan continued, "I am tired of you blaming me every time we get lost. You're a fully capable person. You figure out where we are!"

"Are you serious? That's not very manly to not protect your woman." I began walking back toward the entrance of the subway. "Let's at least get out of here, and we can figure out where we're going once we're back on the subway." I huffed back to the gate and descended the stairs, past the homeless group huddled in the corner.

"Jess," Ryan grabbed my arm, "I do want to keep you safe, but I am not good with directions; you know this. If you can be patient,

LOVIN' WITH GRIT & GRACE

I'll try to figure it out, but don't make this a big deal because I don't need an argument on top of everything else."

"Fine," I agreed and then whispered, "but I still think it's the man's job to keep his wife safe."

"I DO TOO!" he yelled, tired and over it at this point.

Once back on the subway, we both slumped into our chairs.

"Why don't you just ask someone?" I questioned my husband

"Because I can figure it out."

"I know you can, but wouldn't it be so much easier to ask?"

"You ask if you don't trust me."

"I do trust you, but I'm ready to get home."

I set aside my magazine and turned to the older gentleman sitting beside me.

"Excuse me, sir, we need to get to Martin Luther King Jr. Street in Brooklyn. Do you know what exit we need?"

"Yeah, you need the red line. You're on the yellow line. Next stop, get off and find the red line going South."

"Thank you!" I replied and then turned to tell my husband the good news that we had been rescued.

An hour later, we finally arrived home and plopped down on the couch to decompress before calling it a night. I was still irritated when Ryan turned to me.

"Jess, I want to keep you safe. There is nothing I want more; but you need to understand, I don't know New York City, and I'm not good with directions. I'll spend some time tomorrow getting familiar with the subway lines so this doesn't happen again, but you have to cut me some slack. Just because 'men are supposed to keep women safe' doesn't mean we automatically know how to get from point A to point B."

"I know," I replied, "but I don't understand why men have such a hard time asking for help."

126

"Because we don't want to look incompetent. It is our greatest fear to be viewed as a failure, and when we can't come through for our wives, that's really hard on us."

"Okay." I snuggled up to him, ready to put the day behind us and start fresh the next morning.

"I'll try to remember to give you more grace when it comes to directions, and maybe you try to reach out for help more often."

He smiled. "Deal; and you try to remember to keep your opinions to a minimum."

Money Problems

Ryan and I generally see eye to eye on most money matters—remember, we're both cheap—but we aren't exempt from the occasional disagreement.

We've been building a house for what seems like an eternity this past year. By the time this book hits the world, we will have lived in our accessible dream home for about a year! I can't wait! However, in the here and now, our progress has been stalled repeatedly due to COVID, sick contractors, and supply shortages. This impediment has led to our 0 percent construction loan expiring, which means we now have to pay interest on a house we don't live in, which neither of us is excited about. These interest payments have led to a cash-flow snag. We still have a savings account, but it is quickly dwindling, and that causes anxiety. I get panicky when we don't have a nice big cushion, as I am immediately transported back to a time of financial difficulty when Jason couldn't work because of cancer treatments, and we could hardly afford food for our growing family. A time when I often sold possessions to buy necessities or pay the electric bill. A time when the heat was set at 65 degrees, and I was always cold. A time I never want to revisit.

A few days ago, Ryan mentioned he wanted to discuss a potential purchase. We only discuss purchases when they are quite large.

I agreed but was hesitant as I was aware that our bank account wasn't as cushioned as I would like it to be.

We sat down on my bed together, and he began: "Honey, we need to consider purchasing a snowblower asap. The contractors are frustrated because they're always getting stuck in our driveway, and the snow doesn't look like it's going anywhere anytime soon. What do you think?"

I asked, "How much are we talking about?" I wanted a dollar amount before committing to anything.

"Probably around $1,000," he responded.

"$1,000?!" I asked, shocked. "Don't you think you could find something used for half that amount?"

"I don't want used," he replied. "I hate working on things that break all the time, and I want something new with a warranty."

"Can't you look for a good used one?" I continued. "Maybe check Facebook marketplace and Craigslist? You never know."

"You can look," he continued, "but I don't have time."

We sat silent, neither willing to budge. "Okay, I'll check on our options tomorrow," I said as I slowly rose.

I did check the next day and had no idea what I was looking for. I sent a text with a few options to my husband, and he immediately shot them down as "not what he wanted."

Neither of us made another move for about a week, and then I received a call while meandering the aisles of a local thrift store.

"Hey, babe," my husband began, "I wanted your blessing to buy this snowblower that's on sale, and I'll get an 11-percent rebate back."

"How much?" I asked.

"$700," he responded.

"I guess," I replied, "but do I have your word that we'll both reign in our spending while we have this interest loan to pay?

No more fast-food lunches and expensive date nights. Let's both commit, okay?"

He agreed. He made the purchase, and now we're all happier that we're not getting stuck in our driveway anymore.

How is your money situation? Like I mentioned, this usually isn't an area of contention for us, but every once in a while, one of us will have a big purchase in mind and the other won't be excited about spending that amount of money. Again, communication is key, and maybe taking a pause like we did can help. If Ryan had really pushed the issue from the get-go, I probably would have dug in my heels, but he waited. I looked and wrapped my mind around the cost, and then I was okay proceeding with the brand-new option that was on sale.

Here are a few financial rules we try to live by:

- Budget. Not fun or sexy but it works. I have a friend who loves to shop. This trait almost led to a divorce until her husband budgeted her a specific amount of money every month and said, "Do as you please with it. When it's gone, it's gone." This system works for them.
- We eat most of our meals at home, which saves a lot of money with our big family.
- We also pay cash for almost everything, including our older vehicles, which seem to cause our children embarrassment, but we don't care.
- We've cut out money suckers like numerous television options. Who really needs Netflix, Disney Plus, Amazon Prime, and Hulu?
- Communicate. Again, this is so important because we need to be on the same team when it comes to finances or it will blow up in our faces.

Remember Me? When a Parent Forgets They're a Spouse

I have seen this scenario play out a million times, well, maybe not that many, but it is common and toxic. Girl and boy fall in love and get married. They adore each other for the first few years. They establish their roles within the relationship, they travel, have fun date nights, explore new hobbies, and maybe adopt a puppy, and then one of them (usually the girl) wants to have a baby. They get pregnant, have the child, and then the girl forgets that along with being a mother, she is also a wife. Instead of prioritizing the relationship with her husband—the man she once couldn't get enough of—she now only has eyes for the baby. Her love, affection, and desire for him are replaced with this new life they have created. For a certain amount of time, most men are tolerant of this arrangement because, yes, newborn babies require a ton of energy, and yes, moms are exhausted and are not necessarily in the mood for extracurriculars like date night or sex. However, as time marches forward, and the baby grows and more children are added to the brood, one day the boy and girl who adored one another realize they no longer have a relationship outside of the children because they haven't cultivated anything with one another for years! I'm using the mom as the example here, but I have seen it play out with dads too who pour every ounce of energy into their children or job, and the wife is left wondering, *what happened to his desire for me?*

One of my best friends grew up in a large family like I did and was also the oldest of many siblings. We met in seventh grade and there was an immediate connection because of our similarities. We hung out every chance we could, and often these playdates occurred at her house, where I became intimately aware of the inner workings of her family dynamics. One thing that struck me as a young thirteen-year-old was how close her parents were to each other after years of marriage and multiple children. Every day, when her dad returned home from work, he and his wife would retreat to their bedroom for ten to fifteen minutes to catch up on the day. I'm sure she unloaded her frustrations as a stay-at-home mom, and he unloaded his frustrations as the bread winner. They eventually emerged from their bedroom with smiles. I also found it interesting that the wife was extremely devoted to keeping herself fit and attractive for her husband and could often be found working out or pampering herself with spa appointments. They never missed a date night and to this day, have maintained the important tradition of pursuing one another. As an outsider and as a child, the perception I had was that the marriage took top priority and the children followed. These were good parents who did not neglect their children, but the relationship between husband and wife was the priority, and in doing this, they created a forever home for their family. That's a gift with no monetary value. To know as a grown child that there is a home for you where your parents still love and cherish one another is a gift of immense value. And a rare gift according to a 2020 survey that recently reported that only 40 percent of families today are comprised of a married mom and dad.[1]

Ryan's Take

My dad wasn't in the picture much when I was growing up, so I wasn't able to witness firsthand what marriage looked like and what the role of a husband was. I don't remember seeing anybody else get it right, so it's been quite a learning curve for me in my marriages. The phrase "happy wife, happy life" has always resonated, but it's not a natural occurrence for most relationships. It takes work! I do know that I have noticed many marriages where the husband is put on the back burner, and I appreciate that Jess does not operate like this. From the day we married, I have been and have felt like a top priority to her, and I know that couldn't have been easy, especially as a mom to four children—four children who were grieving, and one who had special needs. Speaking as a man, I know that when a wife shoves her husband out of the picture, a man will often find fulfillment in work, or he'll begin to seek fulfillment in unhealthy places like pornography or within an affair. Men are really pretty simple. We want to be seen and desired by our wives, and nine times out of ten, if we are, we are happy and content.

Sometimes the household nitty-gritty is simply about setting aside a few moments to connect with your spouse. It can be like my friend's parents as they prioritized these moments after work, or maybe it's meeting your spouse for coffee or lunch during the week. It's the daily choices that create our life together. Consider your relationship. What is one change you could make to prioritize the marriage? Jot it down here and then make it a top priority in the coming days.

Summer Walks

It's June here in Michigan, and the weather is simply beautiful. I'm truly a Northern girl at heart, and living in the South took a toll on me with the hot Southern sun beating down throughout the long summer months, which caused my walks to be less about enjoyment and more about time spent in a literal sauna sweating out every toxin in my body. I'm excited to see snow again after seven years of being without! I'm also excited to have the heat of the Northern sun disrupted by the cool, crisp breeze that living near Lake Michigan provides. One of our favorite lake towns to visit is Grand Haven, which sits right on the water and is only a few miles from our new house. Grand Haven is a quaint little town—quiet throughout the cooler winter months but come summertime, watch out! It is a hot vacation spot and people swarm upon this sleepy little town to appreciate the beauty of the lake, enjoy long walks on the pier, and savor tasty ice-cream cones from one of the local vendors.

When Mabel, Lucas, and I first moved, I felt out of sorts. I missed my husband and my other children, and my remedy was to keep moving, as I figured the days would go faster and then I'd have my family back under one roof before I knew it. This was also my strategy during pregnancy: keep moving and the baby will be out before you know it!

One restless evening, I took the kids to Grand Haven for a walk. Mabel was helpful in gathering the supplies needed to take Lucas—change of clothes, extra diapers, wipes, two sippy cups of apple juice, stroller, and snacks—and we were ready to go!

Normally, it would be difficult to find a parking space on a crowded summer night in Grand Haven, but one of the perks of bringing Lucas is being able to use his handicapped decal, and Grand Haven is one of the best places I have ever been for accessibility. We shimmied into a tight spot, right next to the playground, which Lucas noticed and requested loudly, "GO WHEE! GO SLIDE! GO WHEE!" So we agreed, and Lucas enjoyed playing for five minutes.

Next, we coaxed him into his stroller and began to walk. We went walking up and down the pier, stopping to tie his shoes, leaning into patience when he screamed "ALL DONE," allowing him to exit his stroller and lean on my arms as Mabel charged ahead with the stroller, which led to an exercise in holding my tongue as children asked their parents, "What's wrong with him?"

Having a child with disabilities has taught me lessons in grace, patience, and kindness. Watching Lucas be so determined to walk, which he can only accomplish with assistance, watching him take one step after another, leaning on me when he requires support, has taught me that it's okay to lean on others, including my husband when I'm weary. It's okay to allow Ryan's strength to carry me for a while. Being a special needs caregiver has taught me invaluable lessons about humility and setting aside my agenda. Once I have my mind made up about something, it is hard to sway me to look at the issue differently; but the special needs caregiver community constantly asks: What could we do differently to include this child? To accommodate this family? To serve this individual as Christ served?

I know many people look upon us with pity, but they don't understand that our responses to experiences like these bring glory to God. These children are the people Christ served here on earth, and they are the most proficient instruments that the Lord will use to chip away any pride, selfish ambition, or greed. The Lucases of the world are the gateway to Heaven, and it is my honor to raise him for the Glory of the King.

What in your life do you need to reframe through an eternal lens? Maybe it's raising a child with special needs or caring for your husband's mother while ALS eats away at her memory. Maybe it's stepping away from a career to homeschool. Whatever it is, consider the calling through the lens of eternity. Consider what Jesus would say. My bet is he would say, well done, good and faithful servant. Well done.

NOTE

[1] Mike Friedrich, "Census Bureau Releases New Estimates on America's Families and Living Arrangements," U.S. Census Bureau, December 2, 2020, https://www.census.gov/newsroom/press-releases/2020/estimates-families-living-arrangements.html.

5

EXCITEMENT

Required to Thrive—but How?

For any marriage to thrive, someone has to stoke the fire, poke the embers, and send them dancing into the night sky, and then someone needs to throw another log on before the ashes are snuffed out. In other words, one or both of you has to suggest adding a bit of excitement to the daily grind or it becomes exactly that: the daily grind.

Avoiding the grind might look like prioritizing a date night, which, by the way, doesn't have to be expensive. It might include adding a little fun to the mix with the introduction of a new family hobby! Perhaps it's stepping out of your comfort zone and scheduling a massage with a Groupon coupon—a deal that turns out to be "too good to be true"—and then laughing as you relive the memories together. Excitement involves celebrating important milestones like anniversaries and birthdays, crossing items off the bucket list, and then making a revised list! It's dreaming together, and once those dreams come to fruition, coming up with new dreams! Or sneaking off and getting married before your actual wedding day! Yep, we sure did, and we don't regret our decision one bit.

It's not the pursuit of *Super Wow!* every moment of every day—no one can withstand that pressure—but it is finding those small pockets of time where you laugh, dream, and grow because these fun times turn into memories and memories are what solidify a relationship in the long run. Memories are what you remember as your time on earth comes to an end.

Let's start off with something easy like date night. Most couples yearn for this activity but struggle to make it a priority. Maybe I can help a bit with a few suggestions that have worked for us.

Date Night!

"You want to go out tonight?" Ryan recently asked on a lazy Saturday afternoon. Our morning had consisted of a three-mile hike and running a few errands before we rushed home to feed the kids a lunch of mac and cheese, fruit, and potato chips. Finally, the lunch mess was put away, table and counters wiped down, and the remaining crumbs swept into the wastebasket. I tried to relax for a few minutes before something inevitably stole my attention away from relaxing, like my husband when he asked, "You want to go out tonight?"

"I don't know," I responded. "I'm pretty worn out and not sure I want to shower, get ready, put makeup on, and fix my hair. I want to spend time with you, but I'm not sure I have the energy to put forth that much effort," I laughed.

"What if we do pizza and wine at our homestead?" he suggested. "Then you wouldn't have to do anything but show up." He winked.

"Perfect," I responded. "Sounds like my kind of night."

I heated up leftovers for the kids while Ryan ran out to prep our construction site for a night of romantic, childfree bliss.

I fed the kids, Ryan bathed Lucas, we hired one of our big girls to hold down the fort, and off we went, ten minutes away, in sweatpants and tennis shoes, to enjoy the solitude of our future home.

I bounced up the stairs and was pleasantly surprised to find that not only had my husband bought a nice bottle of wine, but he had also outfitted the bistro table with a fresh bouquet of flowers and set it up where we could enjoy the beauty of our secluded backyard.

"This is perfect," I whispered as we sat down, slowly exhaling the stress of the day, and sipping chardonnay while we watched a mama deer and her three babies tentatively saunter into our backyard. We topped off our evening with a walk around our property and collected pine needles for a tea I was excited to make (more on that below).

We realized early on in our marriage that if we were going to make it as a couple, we had to prioritize date night. We understood that our marital success would be found in one-on-one time together; however, finding the time and the energy needed wasn't our only challenge. Finding date night funding was also an issue. We live by a budget, and I am admittedly a finicky eater. I tend to eat pretty clean and have lots of stomach issues if I sacrifice clean food for junk, and in order to eat clean on date night, we typically have to spend the big bucks. Add an appetizer, wine, and maybe split a dessert, and we could easily be looking at a $100 tab for a nice night out on the town. For special occasions, yes, totally worth it. For a weekly date night? Not in our budget. So we've managed to get creative and find affordable options where we can still spend time together but not break the bank. One of our most memorable date nights occurred for $20 in our backyard in the middle of a global lockdown, which I'll share about next.

Yes, it sounds ridiculous. Yes, I am a bit crunchy at heart. Yes, I made this and it's not great, but it is extremely healthy. You see, I read about how pine needle tea has five times the vitamin C content of an orange, and living in the age of COVID, we need as much vitamin C as we can get. I thought, let's try it!

First, it is very important that you find the right kind of pine needles. Our land is abundantly supplied in these. You want the kind where when you rip off one little bundle, it holds five long needles—to make sure, maybe check out a YouTube video on the subject. Next, boil water and then crunch up a bunch of pine needles and place them in the bottom of a mug. Pour the boiling water over the needles and allow them to steep for a few minutes. Sip and enjoy (and even if you don't particularly like the taste, it's still good for you, so count that in your favor).

Affordable and Unique Options

Money should not deter anyone from spending time with their spouse. We have gone through times of feast, famine, and lockdowns, but we have mostly managed to keep our weekly date night a priority. Here are a few suggestions:

- When the world went into lockdown, Ryan and I got creative to escape our zoo-like atmosphere and used our travel trailer, which was parked in the backyard, for a weekly date night. Bottle of wine, food delivery, and a movie, and we were set for a few hours while an older child kept the peace indoors.
- Saturday morning hikes have been a nice way for us to connect, get a workout in, and enjoy some solitude. Sure, our depleted calories are immediately replaced with lattes and bagels, but it's the time together that counts, right?

- We've had many dates on our patio during the early years of Annabelle's life because it was easier to stay home and put her older sister in charge for an hour while we grilled pizzas.
- We love our hot tub dates (or bathtub works well too). Honestly, there is not a child alive who wants to be anywhere near the bathroom if they think their parents are bathing together. Trust me.
- There are tons of Groupon and Community Saver deals that offer buy one/get one deals, and if you have an older child you can hire for babysitting or a grandparent who could perhaps do it for free, you're out of the house for $20 or so.
- You can also barter with another couple. We've never done this, but I have friends who have. One week, one couple watches the kids while the other couple enjoys a night on the town, and then they swap the following week.

One of our favorite dinners is homemade pizza. In my last book, *Blended with Grit and Grace*, I included my perfected pizza dough recipe. Here I'm going to offer an easy version of our favorite grilled BBQ chicken pizza with a few of our favorite store-bought crust options for an easy, somewhat healthy version of a fancy bistro pizza.

BBQ Chicken Pizza

- 2 of my favorite quick and easy crust options:
  - Cauliflower crusts found in the freezer section are a good gluten-free option
  - Essential Baking Co Organic Artisan Thin Crust Pizza Crust

- 1 large red onion, sauteed in olive oil until soft
- Cooked chicken cut in small pieces
- Your favorite BBQ sauce
- Spinach
- Mozzarella cheese
- Parmesan cheese

Preheat the oven (or grill) to 425° F. To assemble: Spread a small amount of sauce over the pizza crust. Add toppings and cheese. Bake for 10-15 minutes (but watch closely).

Secret Excitement

Shhhhh . . . I have a secret to share. A secret that many of our loved ones are still not aware of. A secret we kept from the whole world—except for our children and one other couple. Are you ready? Ryan and I were not officially married on May 29, 2010, in a beautiful, one-hundred-year-old church, as the images in our wedding pictures portray. Nope. Ryan and I ran away to the courthouse on April 22, 2010—one month before our official wedding day!—to get married in secret, and then we enjoyed a secret "mini" honeymoon at the local Hilton Suites.

Why didn't we wait, you might wonder; and honestly, I wonder the same thing at times. I was living in my house with my four children, and Ryan was living in our new home with his three children. Every day, I would retrieve children from bus stops, pick up kids from school, get supplies, make meals, and then go back to Ryan's at night to enjoy dinner together. Then there were baths, a trip back to my house to put the kids to bed, and late-night phone calls with my fiancé who lived twenty minutes away. Instead of a phone call, I really wanted to snuggle on the couch and watch a movie with this man I was about to marry. Yes, we could have waited, but we were so sick of being patient.

We were sick of not living life to the fullest. We were sick of not falling asleep in each other's arms. And we were sick of the added struggles because we were trying to model certain behaviors to our seven young children, and these behaviors included not living together before we were officially married. On April 22, 2011, we looked at each other, and I asked, "Do you want to get married at the courthouse?" He said yes, and so we did. One of the craziest, most out-of-character things either of us had ever done; but if the deaths of our spouses had taught us anything, it was that life is short and to live every day to the fullest, and that's what we intended to do.

We arrived in jeans and T-shirts; our friends stood beside us; we vowed to love, honor, and cherish one another till death do us part; and then we drove off to the Hilton Hotel where we could indulge in some true marital bliss. And I don't regret it for a second.

And the best part? When we arrived home, we called our kids into the family room and told them we had something really exciting to share.

Ryan began.

"Kids, we have exciting news!"

"WHAT?" they asked. "Did you buy us a dog? A hamster? A rabbit? Are we moving again? Are we going to Disney World?"

They held their breath in eager anticipation as Ryan announced: "We secretly got married this past weekend!"

We looked at one another with huge grins.

And then turned to look at the kids who were not impressed.

Caleb was the first to speak: "That's the surprise? I thought you were already married."

And the rest of the crew followed—chiming in with their disappointment:

"That's not a great surprise."

"We thought it was going to be way better, like you got us a dog or we were going to Disney World or something fun."

"Why would getting married be exciting? It's like you've already been married cuz Mom has a ring . . ."

"Fine, maybe you aren't as excited as we are," Dad continued, "but now we're a real family and . . ." I had no idea what was coming after this. "Because we're a real family, we're going to do something fun next weekend!"

Good save, I thought, glancing over at my new husband and wondering what the big surprise was going to be next week.

"WHAT?! WHERE ARE WE GOING?"

Their excitement was back, and we had one shot to redeem ourselves.

"We're going to . . . A BOUNCE HOUSE!" Ryan blurted out and then looked at me, beseeching me to please go along with the plan.

"Yes!" I agreed. "That bounce house that you've all wanted to go to by the YMCA! Dad and I thought we'd bring you there!"

"YAY!" Excited exclamations ensued along with hurried conversations about how much fun *next* weekend was going to be.

I cozied up to my new husband with a contented smile. The kids might have fun next weekend, but my new husband and I had already had our moment. Now we were committed to having fun for as many weekends as the Lord saw fit to give our new family.

Step Out of Your Comfort Zone!

While searching for the perfect land to build our house on, Ryan and I wanted to rely less on vehicles and more on walking and biking. Part of this had to do with getting older, which included more difficulties staying in shape due to lagging metabolism, time, children . . . pick an excuse and we have it. Part of it had to do with wanting to utilize this huge bike trailer we have for Lucas that rarely gets used, and part of it had to do with being more environmentally conscious.

Our number one criterion was easy access to bike paths that led somewhere: restaurants, grocery stores, library, church, something. I found a piece of property, and our builder met me there. This four-acre parcel seemed perfect. It had bike paths for miles. It was a mile away from Lake Michigan. It was stunningly beautiful and secluded. The builder walked it and said it was perfect. We bought it (along with all the wetland issues we would encounter later that would deem it "not as perfect"; but God was faithful, and we were able to use it).

Now that we had a future home with bike trails, we needed to go bike shopping! It's not that I don't know how to ride a bike, because I do; it's just when I ride a bike, my body pays for the activity for days after. My rear end aches. My back aches from leaning over. I don't understand the purpose of "just riding a bike." I get riding to a destination like the library or a coffee shop but to simply ride and then deal with the agony of how my body feels later seems kind of pointless. However, Ryan really wanted to do this as a hobby together.

On our first day bike shopping, we stopped at a popular store in town. We walked in to discover a completely empty store. Apparently, COVID had done a number on bike production, and lots of people had had a similar idea! We struck out at the second store as well.

"Maybe we're not supposed to be bike people," I whispered to my husband as we left. "Seems odd that bike stores are sold out!"

"Let's check online when we get home," he suggested.

We did, and thankfully Amazon carried all the bikes we could ever want. We each placed an order, and I also ordered the thickest padded bike seat cover I could find, the thickest padded bike shorts I could find, a cute little basket to carry any little trinkets I might find, and finally, a portable freezer to attach to the back of my bike because I thought, *Sure, I'll step out of my comfort zone and ride a bike, but I want to ride our bikes to a park where we can have a romantic picnic together.*

I'm all about the romance.

And we did exactly that. It was a beautiful, sweaty, aching-booty affair. Just because your rear end is padded with all the things doesn't mean your tush isn't going to hurt after a ten-mile ride. Thankfully, I had my ice cooler, and we were able to enjoy chilled beverages, cheese, and crackers as a reward before we got back on our bikes and headed home. Ouch.

I do enjoy trying new things, especially with Ryan. The bike riding has probably been one of our more ambitious endeavors lately, as our typical excursions outside of our comfort zone usually look like making weird teas or foraging for mushrooms. Before you know it, we'll be bird-watching—you know, simple, nonpainful activities for the aging population.

I also appreciate that Ryan will try almost anything at least once. He's taken dance lessons, rock climbing, and cooking classes. Jot down a few options that you and your spouse might try in the next few months, and then do it! Relationships need a consistent pump of fresh ideas to keep the embers hot.

When a Date Becomes a Horror Story

Ryan and I love a good couple's massage—so much so that it's our go-to activity whenever we plan a getaway. We hop on Google and find the best somewhat-affordable option. We've had wonderful experiences full of relaxation, soothing music, and gentle hands . . . and we've had horrific experiences, including a time in Mexico where I'm pretty sure a Spanish-speaking nineteen-year-old took a few too many liberties with my body, and an incident in Nashville where I almost had a panic attack. I was silently lying on the table, waiting, when I heard the owner scream that he was going to kill the masseuse. As this was occurring, I punched out a frantic text to my husband and asked him to not leave because I was terrified. Or there was the experience that takes top billing, which involved a great Groupon deal at an obscure massage parlor. Oh boy. We were in for a treat.

We pulled up to the spa and were slightly concerned. The building was much more dilapidated than the pictures had shown online; however, we checked out the numerous five-star reviews and cautiously walked inside. We had been in shady buildings before and had experienced some of the best massages, including one in China Town. We couldn't understand a word that was said, but wow! Those gifted in the art of Chinese medicine know how to give a massage. This place didn't appear to have the same vibe. We were immediately engulfed by a strange smell of microwaved leftovers. The old green carpet was ratty and littered with debris, and the walls were covered with smudges of dirt. We were welcomed by a middle-aged woman who asked for our names and requested the coupon. We gave her both, and I shot my husband a concerned look as he blindly followed her to the back of the building. There, we were met by her husband, a middle-aged man who had huge strands of black wiry hairs protruding from his nose and ears. They allowed us time to strip down to our undergarments and lie upon the massage tables. Now, I don't usually have a problem speaking up or even causing a scene if I don't feel comfortable, but my husband gets a bit panicky if I do this, and I try to respect this personality trait.

"Honey," I whispered, "this place is gross!"

"Shhhh," he replied. "They're probably listening to you."

"I don't care!"

Creak, the door began to open.

"All set?" asked a deep voice. The nose hair guy had returned.

"I think so," I timidly replied.

"Alrighty then. So who likes a firm touch?"

"That would be Jess," my husband quickly suggested.

"Okay, then Jess gets me!" replied the middle-aged man.

Yay, I thought and stuffed my face into the pillow where I tried to relax and forget about where I was.

The situation quickly went from bad to worse. The man talked the entire time, usually in my ear with his long nose hairs swishing against my neck. I literally had goosebumps, and not in a good way.

Meanwhile, my dear, dear husband, who didn't want to cause a scene, endured his massage from the woman, who audibly passed gas as she touched his body. At one point, she ran out of the room clutching her bottom as she (hopefully) made it to the restroom on time. We shall never know. Lord, have mercy.

That experience, although horrific, has given us a memory we will never ever forget and taught us a valuable lesson. Don't ever purchase buy one/get one free coupons for massages. It's not a good idea unless you're after a story that'll make your friends and family laugh for years to come.

Dream a Little Dream with Me

The year was 2011. Ryan and I were recently married and had purchased a big house on ten acres and settled into life as a new, blended family. It was a nice house; it was a nice life; but we both felt like something was missing, and we began to dream together. Dream of a different life. I remember one conversation in which we envisioned a mountaintop home in the vast expanse of Colorado where we lived out our days making homemade pizza and raising our seven beautiful children. However, as we searched for options, that Colorado dream turned into a rural Tennessee dream when we realized the South offered more affordable options for our large family. Most thought we were crazy to pursue this new life with our kit and caboodle, and maybe we were a little bit, but we yearned for something that was ours, and we took tangible steps to make it a reality.

We dreamt of lots of land with a big house and sprawling hills and a river, and miraculously, we found it! In 2013, we landed in Bath Springs, Tennessee, with a 6,000 square foot home that needed total renovation. A home that overlooked the Tennessee River and was nestled in the hills. We set to work on our dream, tilling the red clay earth, creating gardens, planting a vineyard and fruit trees, canning and freezing and preserving the fruit of our labor. We loved our time on the land and soaked up every amazing experience, and then one day, that dream didn't work anymore, and we began to explore new dreams.

We spent months traveling back and forth to Michigan looking for land to build our new dream of an accessible house. We thrifted on the weekends and purchased great deals at Goodwill and Restore, and often stopped at this little sandwich shop where we ordered cheesy broccoli soup and sandwiches.

As our new house has begun to take shape, we dream of making our home a sanctuary of peace, and we've set it up this way with spaces for the introverted souls to retreat and regroup. We dream of a backyard full of chickens, pigs, gardens, a sauna, and grapevines. I gotta have the vines. Dreaming together has kept the excitement alive and gives us a united purpose as we have worked toward these goals we envision for our family.

Lately, we dream of launching our kids out into the world, and we try to figure out what this looks like for Lucas, who will require care for the rest of his life. Our ideal scenario includes a beautiful farm community where he has purpose, friends, and meaning. We may create this for him, or maybe it will fall into our lap somewhere. My perfect scenario includes a home with numerous bedrooms and bathrooms and a large living space, with pigs and chickens and gardens in the backyard. Activities that would bring meaning and purpose to his life and those he lives with.

I recently took a walk through the unfinished basement in our new house and noticed something. We have already built a version of our dream for Lucas. Our basement is that large open space surrounded by bedrooms and bathrooms. Our backyard will have chickens, pigs, and gardens. I've learned not to project any limitations onto my dreams, and what this really means is that I won't put God in a box. I'm open if the Lord calls us to open our basement for Lucas and those like him. Only time will tell; but in the meantime, it sure is fun to dream about it.

Cheesy Broccoli Soup

We often enjoyed cheesy broccoli soup as we were out thrifting for deals. I don't handle dairy well (therefore, it's usually an occasional treat) and managed to create this fantastic dairy free version. Enjoy.

- 1 Tbsp olive oil
- 1 yellow onion, diced
- 2 bags frozen broccoli (10 oz each)
- 2 peeled garlic cloves, minced
- 4-5 cups bone broth
- Salt and pepper
- 1 cup raw cashews

Place cashews in a heat-safe bowl and pour boiling water over nuts. Leave uncovered. Wait about an hour—or until cashews soften. Place the nuts in a blender and blend, adding water from the bowl until consistency is smooth and creamy. Set aside. Sauté the onion and garlic in the olive oil in a large pot or Dutch oven. Add the broccoli and bone broth. Cook over medium heat until broccoli is tender. Transfer soup to a blender and blend until smooth. Return to pot or Dutch oven and add salt and pepper to taste, then cook on low until heated through. Add cashew cream and mix thoroughly.

Celebrating Milestones

As I write these words, Ryan and I are spending our first anniversary apart in ten years. I am in Michigan, and he is in Tennessee, and it stinks. After loving and losing, I strive to live each day as if it were my last, and part of that motto is spending time with my husband and truly embracing the gift we have together; and right now, I hate missing so many moments. As they say, absence makes the heart grow fonder, and I'm sure fond of this guy.

It's also surreal to realize that I've now been married to Ryan as long as I was married to Jason. I don't take these marriage relationships I've been blessed to have for granted. I'm grateful for every year I have with Ryan beside me; and statistically speaking, it's pretty amazing that we're still standing.

The national statistics claim that 50 percent of first marriages will end in divorce within eight years, 67 percent of second marriages will end in divorce within seven years, and then tack on another 10–25 percent (depending on diagnosis and level of care) probability that a marriage will end in divorce with special needs.[1] That puts my marriage at right around an 8 percent survival rate at best? My goodness.

I'm proud of what we've cultivated in our years together—yes, cultivated. Not sexy or showy, but through hard work, determination, and faith, we have something really worth fighting for. Something many thought would never last.

It's been a lot, for sure. At times we've waded through deep, treacherous paths that threatened to destroy us, every once in a blue moon we found ourselves in the garden of Eden (usually on a beach in Mexico sans the children), but mostly we've worked diligently in a big garden plot full of manure in need of heavy pruning, weeding, and care. We have calloused hands and knees, bug bites, dirty brows, and sun scorched foreheads (we'll blame the wrinkles on that), but we keep going; we keep turning over the compost pile; we keep showing up year after year for the tedious work involved: planting and weeding and watering and reaping our harvest—God willing.

Ryan, I love you with all of me. I'm thankful for your constant presence of calm dedication. I'm thankful we're both loyal to the call. You are the quiet cool flow of water to my blazing passionate sun—both needed for the growth of something beautiful.

Ryan's Take

I couldn't have written it better myself. Losing a spouse has definitely changed the way I feel about anniversaries and everything else. I view life differently and have learned to appreciate it for what it is, a gift. Yes, a gift from God each and every day. Some days I'd like a redo, and some days fly by faster than others, but for the most part, I value each breath I'm given. I'm not the best at showing Jess how much I appreciate her, but occasionally, I let my guard down long enough to say thanks in a way that she feels truly seen. She has taught me so many things and encourages me to be the best I'm meant to be, and every now and then she gives a little nudge, push, or a drop kick to move me in the right direction. I know it's hard to believe, but I can be a little hardheaded as well.

Jess and I have been through a lot in our lives and have had to face some tall mountains within our eleven years of marriage. I love facing it with her beside me because we are meant to be together. I love the quote from Jack Nicholson in the movie *As Good as It Gets*: "You make me want to be a better man." It is true.

I hope those of you reading this have this special bond in your life in your current relationship or are praying God helps you to find this gift in your future. Wanting to be your best is not a given, and finding someone who is willing to watch and wait and encourage that process is priceless. Jess has seen me at my best and at my worst, and she still loves me. That gives me hope and drive to keep striving. It's a win-win. I love her like I have loved no other and look forward to the next fifty years, if God so ordains.

Family Fun

Of course, there's a time and place for marital excitement, but a good marriage also includes fun family times! I loved double Dutch as a young girl and became quite adept at weaving in and out of the jump ropes as they slapped hard against the concrete. When I was twenty-one years old and pursing a teaching degree, I was placed in an urban setting for my student teaching assignment, and the ninth-grade girls were quite impressed with my tall, lanky, blond-hair, blue-eyed girl moves on the double Dutch. So impressed that they begged Ms. Jessica to come outside after school and get in on the action, which I happily obliged. There's nothing like teenage girls experiencing true joy on account of your skills. In other words, they had seriously doubted my ability until I showed up and proved them wrong!

Twenty years later, I got to prove my skills again; skills that were put to the test during the COVID pandemic when we retreated to our homes forever and ever amen. The kids and I brainstormed ways we could keep busy and have fun at home. Ryan and I had set aside some money to make a few online purchases for games, puzzles, and outdoor activities—things that would make our time together more bearable and hopefully enjoyable. It was during this brainstorming session that I was teleported back to my days as a young student teacher wowing the masses with my proficient jumping skills.

"Hey!" I suggested to the crew hunched around me as we scrolled through Amazon. "How about double Dutch jump ropes?"

"What's double Dutch?" asked five-year-old Annabelle.

"Yeah, what's that?" Josh questioned.

"Just a sec." I exited out of Amazon and headed to YouTube to search for a double Dutch video.

I found what I was looking for and pulled up a five-minute video of a couple of young girls crushing it with their jump rope skills.

"See!" I said excitedly. "That's double Dutch!"

"WOW!" Annabelle exclaimed. "They're jumping so fast!"

And they were. The four of us watched mesmerized by the sight we witnessed on the laptop.

"Yes! Let's get double Dutch!" Jada agreed, and just like that, the order was placed. Within a day or two, extremely long jump ropes arrived, and the kids couldn't wait to learn.

That night, after the dinner was put away and the dishes cleared, we headed outside to have some fun. It took a little bit of time to get into the rhythm of the ropes, there is a science to this kind of fun, but once we did, I was the first one up. These youngins needed to be taught a thing or two about jumping ropes.

However, I quickly learned, double Dutch is not like riding a bicycle, and my forty-three-year-old body did not immediately recall my twenty-one-year-old skills!

We fell, we laughed, we picked ourselves back up again and again and again. Even the big kids got in on the action as each tried to one-up the other and stay in the ropes the longest!

We've had lots of fun family moments. We hiked one afternoon and came upon a huge sinkhole. Another time, Josh and Tate found a hidden cavern in our woods and had to show us their finding. We've caught catfish in the river, four wheeled through the cornfields, and fried up crickets. Recently, we purchased a pedal boat because that seemed like a good family activity to pursue on the Great Lake that is just down the road from our new house.

I hope my kids look back fondly on these family memories. As a big family, it is difficult to offer one-on-one time to each child, but I sure hope these collective moments make up for some of those losses. I hope they remember that their mom and dad not only had fun with each other but also made time for fun with them.

NOTE

[1] Jen Thorpe, "Divorce Rate Higher among Couples with Special Needs Children," Familes.com, accessed July 15, 2022, https://www.families.com/divorce-rate-higher-among-couples-with-special-needs-children.

6

ROMANCE

For Women and Men? Let's Find Out

Romance. Women yearn for it, and men often run from it! At least that's been my experience once my man said I do. Why is this? Because I don't believe it's intentional. Ryan isn't thinking, *It would be fun to make my wife feel miserable and unloved by not romancing her for a while.* I actually don't think romance crosses Ryan's radar at all! Instead, I'm pretty sure the lack of romance I feel boils down to communication and misunderstanding.

Early on, Ryan didn't understand how important romance was to me and what exactly was required of him for me to feel romanced. Instead of asking, he simply avoided it altogether. This avoidance became a problem because he married a passionate woman who requires romance like oxygen! When I called him out on this problem during our "relaxing getaway," his response was that he thought he was being romantic by doing the dishes! Oh boy. It took a blowout fight to peel away our misunderstandings and reveal exactly what this concept meant to each of us and our relationship. We also had a conversation about how he could make an effort to maintain consistent romance because, come to find out, he doesn't require romance at all!

I doubt I'm the only wife in the world who desires more of an effort from her husband when it comes to this hot-button topic; in fact, I know I'm not because I've had conversations with close friends who agree. The one thing we don't necessarily agree on is what this looks like in our relationships. One friend wishes her husband would do the dishes more often because this turns her on. Another friend longs for deep talks before she can get in the mood. And, well, yours truly can admittedly be a bit all over the place with romance requirements. I can tell you one thing: I don't hate flowers, and I wouldn't mind having them magically appear a bit more often than they do.

Romantic Misconceptions

February 15, 2014. It was 9:00 a.m. I rolled over as I lovingly beheld the man I had married three years earlier. I fondly recalled the previous day: a day of passion and fine dining, a day saturated in romance with massages, dark chocolate, and red roses and finishing in all-night, passionate love making. A day of pure bliss—an imaginary day and a total crock.

The day actually began when I rolled over and moaned, "Ooohhhhhh," holding my sensitive stomach while glancing at the clock that said 8:00 a.m., which meant it was time to rise and shine after surviving a long night wrought with agony and vomit. The day after Valentine's Day. A day when statistically more people search for a divorce lawyer than any other day of the year. Interesting, eh?

The previous day began innocently enough in plush accommodations, the last leg of an adventurous journey home from what was generally a restful and relaxing vacation for two in the Caribbean. Earlier that morning, I awoke feeling like I had been punched in the gut, a familiar feeling since being diagnosed with food poisoning a few days earlier.

The clock now registered 8:30, and my stomach retched again, indicating that today, as it had been with the previous two days, was going to be a long day. Although I had an appetite, my digestive regions paid for it when I attempted to eat.

My dear, loving husband, eyes closed, asked, "Stomach still hurting, hon?"

"Mm hm," I replied, slowly easing my body to the edge of the mattress as I waited for the pain to pass. I contemplated the price I might pay by ingesting a cup of coffee to offset an oncoming headache and then noticed Ryan had beat me to the pot, which gurgled to life.

We managed to make it to the lobby on time for the complimentary breakfast, and I considered the selections: waffles, eggs, hash browns, and donuts. I chose yogurt with an accompaniment of bacon, because heck, it was Valentine's Day, and I should be allowed to celebrate with something pink and sexy, right?

After breakfast, we continued our embarkment toward home and stopped to pick up groceries to replenish what had been used while we were gone. We ventured into the local Publix and meandered through the aisles, surveying the freshly baked homemade goods, the balloons, the candy, and the red roses, and then my husband grew pale as the sights triggered the meaning behind this day—Valentine's Day—and like a deer in headlights, he began to look to and fro as the situation descended upon him. He did the only thing a man in his position could possibly do and asked, "Honey, do you want to pick out flowers for Valentine's Day?"

I responded, "I'm good, but thanks."

And then we both went silent.

Dead quiet as the various loaves of French bread beside the vast array of flowers suddenly became the most interesting thing either one of us had ever seen in our entire lives.

We finished shopping and checked out. A quiet despondency having fallen upon our conversations, and after loading the bags into the car, Ryan attempted an explanation, which only made the situation worse: "I'm sorry, babe. I would have ordered flowers, but we live in the middle of nowhere and people don't want to deliver that far, and, and, and . . ."

I listened as we turned into the parking lot of the doctor's office, our last stop before heading home. I had to have my blood drawn for a miscarriage they continued to monitor. The nurse, the sweetest woman, asked whether we had plans for the BIG DAY, to which I replied, "I'm not sure, but I don't think flowers are involved."

Ryan nervously laughed.

She replied, "Oh I hate flowers anyway. They always die!"

I rolled my eyes as we got up to leave.

Once back in the car, I digressed at length on the philosophical, spiritual, and emotional reasons why any woman would say she hates flowers and how this statement is not only most likely false but also an assault on women everywhere! In fact, I said, pointing my finger at Ryan, the only male within hearing distance, "Women are so disappointed that they have simply given up on Valentine's Day, and in turn, they have disillusioned themselves into believing they actually hate flowers when no woman *hates* flowers."

I let that last statement hang in the air—

"ANNNNDDDD, I continued, your woman especially doesn't hate flowers and would love a small act of appreciation to show that she is special and treasured and remembered and loved on this stupid day."

"Is that all?" Ryan smirked. "Just special and treasured and remembered and loved? That'll cover my bases?"

I turned to look out the window and became very interested in the trees swooshing by.

We finally arrived home to discover the dishwasher and the washing machine had broken while we were gone, and we had exactly one hour to unload the groceries, unpack suitcases, and fix the broken appliances before the kids arrived home from school. Our progress was interrupted with Mya bursting through the door and announcing: "JOSH IS PROJECTILE VOMITING!"

"Welcome home," I murmured under my breath as five human beings burst through the door.

"Mom and Dad, you're home!"

Ryan and I were instantly wrapped in sticky love, candy bags, cards, schoolwork, and a goldfish.

"Who got a goldfish for Valentine's Day?" I questioned holding the bag with the slightly lethargic fish. "Is this one of those Pinterest fads that I missed?"

Why the Ronne family? We can hardly take care of the human beings in our home let alone a goldfish.

"This can't be real," I muttered, and then did what I do in stressful situations and jokingly yelled out, "Honey! Mya brought home dinner!"

I caught Tate's eye, the child who 100 percent appreciates my humor, and we enjoyed a good laugh together.

After the kids devoured a delightful Valentine's Day meal of Campbell's tomato soup and grilled cheese, Ryan and I were able to relax. We sat down to enjoy a romantic meal of rib eye steaks and asparagus and allowed our bodies to embrace peace when BAM!

SPITTER, SPATTER, CRACKLE, WHRILLLLL.

Why not? No dishwasher, no dryer, one child projectile vomiting, four exhausted children, pukey laundry everywhere, dirty vacation laundry still in the luggage, tired and grumpy parents, painful stomachs, and no flowers—of course, the power would go out! Within five minutes we had fifty candles lit, lighting up our home like a Christmas tree. The kids were checked on, everyone accounted for, and as my dear husband poured two glasses of extremely rare, boxed wine, we looked at one another, searching for something in each other's eyes, and we found exactly what we were looking for: love.

It was always there, on this Hallmark day full of exaggerated expectations and false hopes. It was there in the pot of coffee, in the quiet admonishment and eye roll agreements, and in the steak dinner lovingly prepared in the midst of chaos. It was there while we cleaned up puke, and there fixing the appliances after an incredibly long, stressful day. It was there, among those fifty beautifully bright candles, in the question, *Is this our Valentine's Day?* And it will always be there. It is our love story. It was our Valentine's Day, and it held its own version of romance—even without flowers.

- 2 rib eye steaks
- Asparagus
- Olive oil
- Salt and pepper
- Montreal Steak Seasoning
- Dale's Steak Seasoning

Preheat the oven to 350° F. Place the steaks in a shallow pan. Baste both sides of the steaks with Dale's Steak Seasoning. Apply salt, pepper, and Montreal Steak

Seasoning to both sides. Marinate about an hour and then heat a cast iron skillet on medium high. Sear one side of each steak for about 5 minutes (based on taste and thickness of steak). Flip over and cook another 4-5 minutes. Place a tablespoon of butter on top of each steak. Remove and let sit for a few minutes. Place the asparagus in a shallow dish and drizzle with olive oil. Apply salt and pepper. Bake for approximately 10 minutes until al dente (still firm but cooked through).

A Man's Idea of Romance

My husband likes to cuddle, and I do not. In bed, I like my space; however, I know that cuddling makes him feel loved, and I try to accommodate his desire as he inches closer toward me—his perimenopausal wife who is undoubtedly dying of hot flashes.

I've asked him, "Is cuddling how you feel romanced?"

And he's replied, "Not necessarily. I like to be close to you, which is why I like to cuddle. I feel happy when you're happy."

"But is that romance to you?" I prod the issue even further

"I think so," he replies.

"You're happy when I'm happy. I'm not sure how I feel about that because there are a lot of times when I'm not happy!" I nervously laugh at this realization.

Ryan's Take

I'm pretty sure most men want to remove the word "romance" from the English language. It is probably one of the most confusing words for a man, and for any husband telling your wife right now that you don't know what I'm talking about, you can private message me later. I'm no expert, but I bet the majority of marital fights are somehow tied to romance in one way or another. If asked whether I know what romance is, the answer is no. Just no. There is no romance requirement in my life. The issue in my marriage is that I have gotten Jess's expectations right on occasion, so the bar is set high, and then that part of my brain quits working, and I fall flat the next time. Confession time. When I truly put forth the effort required to romance my wife, I typically get it right. Or at least I get partial credit for the attempt. Women appreciate men making the effort to romance them—or at least that's what I've been told. I don't know why we tend to be so lazy in this category because it usually benefits us in a way that fulfills our idea of romance.

Jess wants to feel special. Let me expand that thought: Jess wants to know that I think she is special, and that I desire her and choose to continue to pursue her long after the butterflies have fluttered away. I know there's always room for improvement, and I for sure don't want someone else to fill that gap, so yes, I guess an accurate definition of romance for me is when my wife is happy, I'm happy. It's that simple.

Understanding What Romance Is to the One You Love

I hazily walked to the kitchen one morning, the first day into solo parenting my crew after Ryan had left earlier that morning to work out of town for the week. Yes, we had agreed to this arrangement, but it was still difficult and overwhelming.

I don't sleep well when my husband is out of town, and there are a couple of factors that play into this reality. One, I scroll social media far too late into the night when I don't have Ryan to hold me accountable. When we're together, we head to our bedroom at 8:00, watch our shows until 10:00, and then it's lights out. When my husband is not around, I tend to scroll and call it work. It's not healthy, but it's a coping mechanism. Second, I don't enjoy the pressure of the children's well-being falling solely on me. I double-check the locks at night and send my big boys texts, pleading with them, "Please remember to lock the door when you come home tonight."

And I check Lucas on the baby monitor and sleep with one eye open "just in case." On this particular morning after a fitful night of sleep, I shuffled to the coffee pot where I intended to pour myself a huge cup of joe, and that's when I realized we were out of coconut milk, what I pour into my coffee if I need it to cool off quickly so I can engulf it before heading to Lucas's room to get him ready. As a caregiver to a child with profound special needs who is still in diapers at seventeen years old, I can assure you that I don't like to wade into that scenario before coffee. I don't really like to ever wade into that, especially at 7:00 a.m., but if I have to, I'm going to make sure I'm caffeinated.

I grabbed a pen off Ryan's desk and walked over to the fridge where our grocery list hung. I wrote coconut milk and stopped. Right after bananas there was a sweet message:

Jess, I love you. Hang in there. This will be over before we know it.

The grocery list spoke—or better yet, my husband had thought of me in the wee early morning hours before he headed out—and that simple message was better than any amount of caffeine I could have consumed.

In the first year or two of marriage, we took Gary Chapman's Love Language™ test. The premise is that there are five dominant ways to feel loved, and by taking the test, we have a better understanding of how those in our lives receive and give love. The five ways are words of affirmation, physical touch, receiving gifts, quality time, and acts of service. Ryan tends to lean toward performing acts of service for those he loves, but that's where we misfired for years. I don't feel loved when the dishes are clean or when the laundry is folded and put away. Sure, it's nice to have those chores accomplished, but they don't fill my love tank. Those simply feel like chores that need to be accomplished as a family. After taking the test together, which was extremely eye-opening, we discovered we share the exact same love languages, which made it easy to remember! We are both words of affirmation people with physical touch coming in as a close second. Once Ryan understood this, he was better able to implement what I needed. It's not that I don't appreciate having clean dishes; it's just not an action that's going to make me feel loved.

Since this revelation, I have walked into a steamy bathroom to find those three little words etched upon the mirror. I have seen those words stepping out my front door, etched in sidewalk chalk, and I had been the recipient of lots of notes throughout our early years together.

He was so good at the wooing and loving and romancing part early on in our marriage; but something shifted as our lives became busier and the years added more gray hairs and wrinkles. It didn't seem like my husband cared much anymore, and I never got those sweet little love reminders because he was busy. Instead, his attitude became "he had won me" so why did he have to keep working at it? And that was an attitude I didn't necessarily appreciate.

I Already Got You

"It feels like you don't even make the effort anymore!" I wailed to my husband one Saturday night.

"What?" he questioned.

"We've had this discussion about a hundred times, and you still don't understand. I don't know how to get through to you!"

I walked away, irritated and feeling like I continued to bang my head against a brick wall, and that brick wall happened to be the man I had married. He seemed incapable of understanding what I meant when I suggested he put forth effort into our relationship. I headed to our bedroom to do some yoga and cool off, and he headed to his woodshop to do the same. This had become our go-to method of simultaneously taking a big pause and reflecting on what the other was attempting to communicate. It was also our way of not saying something hurtful we might regret later. We had been down this road before, and there were words in the universe that should have never been said because, honestly, we didn't mean them, and they were simply spouted off in the heat of the moment.

As I half-heartedly engaged in the yoga session on YouTube, my mind swirled. It did seem like Ryan genuinely had no idea what I was saying when I told him he no longer made the effort. I told him time and time again, "I want you to initiate date nights. I want you to surprise me with something special. I want you to show me that you still want and desire me! Somehow!" I had even given him a list (per his request) of thirty ways he could show me that he did care, show me that he was happy with his marital selection; but here we were again. Yes, in the middle of a busy season, again. I understood. I felt just as stressed, but I didn't feel like I was asking for the sun, moon, and stars. I simply wanted an occasional glimpse of the man I had dated, the one who wooed me with poetry, homemade books, and love songs. The one who seemed completely enamored with me. I hadn't seen that guy in a long time, and every time I suggested that maybe he could show up once in a while, the only response I received was, "Jess, I already won. I got you! A man loves the thrill of the chase, and I conquered you."

Yes, he said it with a sly grin, but it didn't make it hurt any less. I wanted a husband who continued to pursue me, continued to chase me, and did not assume I was a one-and-done deal. I understood that we were busy; but I thought "teamwork makes the dream work," and it sure seemed like the busyness of our life would be a lot more bearable if he and I were clicking in a good way.

Ryan's Take

Almost everything in a man's life requires a pursuit with a reward if the objective is accomplished. Okay, so maybe it's not a requirement but more like a preference. Most men love sports. We understand what it takes to achieve greatness on the field or the court; but in life, it's more challenging. I am really good at the initial pursuit (Jess may or may not agree with my evaluation of myself). But all joking aside, most men love the hunt, and then we fall into the trap Jess mentioned earlier. When she said she would marry me, winner, winner, chicken dinner! I threw everything in my arsenal at her and won her, so when this conversation came up in our marriage, I'm sure my jaw dropped. What do you mean, I have to come up with more romantic stuff? I am apparently a bit clueless when it comes to continuing the pursuit. I admittedly hide behind house duties; and recently, our pastor shattered my perspective by pointing out that doing housework and many other things was a form of worship . . . to God. *Woooaaah! Wait a second, that's how I show Jess I love her! Now what?* I wondered. Side note: If you're having marital problems, skip counseling and write a book with your spouse. That'll shine a light on your problems really fast. Just kidding.

Admittedly, I don't pursue my wife like she deserves, and I tend to make excuses for my shortcomings, but here's what I know at forty-four years old: Jess wants to feel loved, and I want her to feel loved. Jess wants to be happy, and I want her to be happy. Jess often tells me exactly what she needs me to do but, for some reason, something in my head replaces her desires with things I would rather do, and then I hope she accepts them instead. Wow! That's a real aha moment for me. Time to sit down with the love of my life and really listen to what she needs from me and change how I show her how valuable she is to me. I take her for granted as do many of you with your significant others, and it's time to make a change. Will you join me? I hope that in Jess's next book she'll be able to brag about how much I have transformed in this particular area.

Fall Walks

The air is brisk
The sun is high
I'm walking beside you
And let out a sigh

A sigh of joy
A sigh of bliss
A sigh to signal
I'd treasure a kiss

You smile at me
As we walk hand in hand
A sign of your love
Committed, we stand.

I love you my dear
And treasure our talks
As we bask in the goodness
Of our fall weather walks.

At our rural house in Bath Springs, Tennessee, we enjoyed roaming our expansive property. Almost daily, I walked up and down our long dusty road, often to meet the kids as they exited the bus, and most days, my eyes would shift to the left as I passed this mountainous hill on our property, a hill I had never climbed, but a hill that mesmerized me nonetheless. I was sure if I could make it to the top of that hill, I would witness a breathtaking view.

One lazy Saturday afternoon, Ryan and I were lounging around the house. Lucas had a caregiver, and the rest of the kids were watching a movie. We contemplated a date night but wondered if we were feeling too worn out from the week.

We went back and forth: yes, it would be nice to get out of the house for a bit, but was it worth the effort? And then I had an idea.

"What if we packed a picnic and hiked up that tall hill at the end of our driveway? I bet it's beautiful up there and probably overlooks the river!"

"You think you're up for that," Ryan questioned, "with your hip issues?"

"Sure," I surmised. "I'll be fine."

"That sounds fun if you can handle it," he responded and changed into his hiking gear while I prepared a backpack for our dinner reservation at the top of whatever we were going to find on that hill. I packed sandwiches, sparkling water, chopped up fruit, and bags of kettle chips. Ryan strapped the backpack to his shoulders, we put Caleb and Tate in charge of watching the younger kids, and off we went to explore the unknown.

Our terrain was rough, tougher than I expected, and Ryan had the bright idea to go around to the back side of the hill and hike it from that vantage point. We first encountered flat land, but it was full of burrs, those pesky, prickly balls that fervently attach themselves to everything they come in contact with. He led with a stick and tried to knock the branches down before my body encountered them, and although helpful, I was still covered in prickly balls by the time we made it through. Next, we stumbled through the wetlands, which we weren't aware existed. Thankfully, we had donned our rubber boots, which made the muck less of a hinderance and more of a squishy gross factor as we continued our excursion. We weaved in and out of the dense forest covered with red, yellow, and brown leaves—signaling a change in seasons was about to be upon us. Finally, we arrived at the base of the mountainous hill, and as my chin lifted to survey what would now be required of me, I began to get nervous that maybe my forty-year-old body wasn't quite as capable as I thought with aching hips after pulling my heavy legs out of a mile worth of wetland gunk. Still, I would not be deterred. I was climbing this hill if it killed me, or my husband would carry me—which was in no way a viable option.

"You ready?" He looked my way. "No turning back once we start!"

He was giddy as he pretended he was Bear Grylls—on date night nonetheless.

"Yep," I sighed. "Let's do it."

And up we went. Step by step up the steepest incline I've ever climbed! Every few minutes I stopped, placed hands on my weary legs, and tried to catch my breath. I stumbled as my foot brushed against an old root, and Ryan reached out to pull me back up. One foot in front of the other as our breath quickened, each determined to make it to the top where we would enjoy the fruits of our labor.

Finally, about sixty minutes later—but it sure felt like much longer!—there were only a few steps remaining. I reached into the deep crevices of my soul to find the strength I needed and heard the lyrics to a familiar song: "What doesn't kill you makes you stronger!"—just the words I needed from Kelly Clarkson to spur me to the end, one step, two steps, three steps. I lurched forward and saw one of the most beautiful sights I had ever seen, right on our property at the top of this painstakingly difficult mountain hill, my eyes beheld breathtaking beauty. Ryan grabbed my hand and we looked around us—standing a hundred plus feet above our homestead, we were surrounded by a field of beautiful wild flowers and the grand Tennessee River flowed below. We spread out the blanket, slumped to the ground, and began diving into our food sources, famished from the long, strenuous hike we had just completed. We ate silently, in awe of the natural beauty that surrounded us from every side. The river gently flowing, the yellow flowers bending to the will of the wind, and a bald eagle circling overhead, curious about the two mysterious creatures who had ventured into his silent territory.

We sat and ate and drank our sparkling waters and soaked in the beauty, and then the sun began to descend, and we knew if we didn't start moving, we would be stuck navigating our way back home in the dark. We packed everything away and began to make our descent back to the flickering lights of home.

That walk is one of my favorite romantic memories. A beautiful fall walk that gave me permission to let go of the dead stuff in our relationship—the petty stuff—maybe even let go of my desire for flowers. But probably not. To recognize the beauty of what I had in the man I had married, not to focus on what he didn't do but instead enjoy time with one another in God's beautiful creation. Accomplishing that difficult hike with Ryan is something I'll never forget. A picnic, a workout, and the beauty of God's creation are apparently the playbook to my soul.

What's the playbook to your soul? Is it something similar? Being out in nature? Date night? Or is it something different? Jot down a few thoughts and then share them with your spouse. Maybe you can accomplish a couple of these romantic ideas in the coming weeks.

Getaways

It was the summer of 2020, and Ryan and I were restless after spending months in lockdown. Restless is an understatement. We needed to get the heck out of dodge and get out quickly before we lost our minds. We didn't care where we went. Honestly, we could have camped out at the local state park, but instead we headed to Helen, Georgia, a quaint getaway in the southern hills of Georgia. We wined and dined and swam and stayed up late and ate too much food and hiked and antiqued and explored the local vineyards. On our last day, we took a meandering drive through the hills to "see what we see"—a little Jessicaism I often say when Ryan is confused about meandering to nowhere.

We climbed into the van, rolled down the windows, and blasted some tunes; not a care in the world. I reached over to check my phone, a habit that dies hard with a bunch of kids, and was surprised to see a message from an online friend whose husband had been battling brain cancer for ten years. He had entered hospice care, and his wife mentioned that the doctors gave him a month to live. He had opted for natural remedies for the majority of those years, and when the natural stopped working, he pursued chemo and radiation. A beautiful human being with a zest for life as showcased when he married Lori and then proceeded to have three daughters, one after another. I read the words in front of me and began to weep. This man who had fought so hard for ten years and had lived so courageously, not allowing cancer to have the final word, was about to exit this world.

Ryan reached over for my hand. "What's wrong?" he asked, and I sputtered out what I had read about David. We sat in silence, the beauty of our marriage, our health, and our ability to be on this getaway together shadowed by the gravity of our friend's situation back in Michigan, a situation Ryan and I were all too familiar with.

That night we prayed for Lori's family, and we thanked the Lord for the time we were able to spend together, time that is never guaranteed and should never be taken for granted. And then in honor of David and Lori and all those fighting battles unseen, we lived our last day in the Georgia mountains to the fullest! We toured a winery and had a picnic. We sat in rocking chairs on our porch and pointed in awe as a bear rummaged through the trash in front of our log cabin. We snuggled together on the couch, comforted by our love for one another. We appreciated the gift of another day, and that's all we can do, right? When we hear news of someone going through a difficult season. Sure, we can pray and help and bring a meal, but then we have to honor their struggle, honor their life by living ours in thankfulness and full of joy; not squandering our time but using the gift of life to lead others to Christ and to do good works for his glory.

That last night together, we made club sandwiches—my go-to whenever I'm in the mood for some gluttonous delights! These are the best; and if wrapped in tin foil, they stay fresh for a bit. Try them. You won't be disappointed.

Turkey Club Sandwiches

- Good quality sourdough bread
- Butter
- A few strips of fried bacon
- Good quality deli roasted turkey
- A few spinach leaves
- A couple of slices of tomatoes
- Mayo
- Swiss or provolone cheese

Slather one side of two pieces of bread with butter and lay the buttered side flat in a skillet. Add the cheese, then the spinach leaves, the turkey, and bacon strips, and top with the second piece of bread. Fry until lightly browned. Remove and add tomatoes and mayo if desired.

Romance Killers

I emerged from the hot tub, soaking wet and freezing cold as the bitter December air hit my skin. I grabbed the closest towel and wrapped my shivering body in the warmth. I walked toward the cozy glow coming from the house; smiling after a nice romantic evening with my husband, when I heard, "Hey! You took my towel!"

"What?" I responded, confused. "There's another towel. Use that one!" I shouted over my shoulder.

"But," he hollered back, "I got that towel for myself!"

"Seriously?" I asked him. "You're going to make me take this towel off and put the other one on? So much for romance." I threw the towel his way as I grabbed the other one and darted inside. "What a jerk," I said under my breath, slamming the door shut behind me.

I hopped into the shower to wash away the chlorine and stewed over Ryan's response. Was he seriously upset that I took his towel? "He better not have any extracurricular activities planned for the evening," I muttered.

I dried off and put my pjs on before heading to our bed to unwind. As I entered our room, I saw my husband pensively sitting on the edge of the bed, dried off with his towel and now in athletic shorts. He looked up as I walked in.

"I'm sorry," he said. "I shouldn't have made the towel such a big deal."

I listened. I had two choices. I could berate him and tell him how stupid it was that he had made such a big deal about a towel and how he probably ruined our night, or I could graciously accept his apology.

I chose the latter. I don't always choose the right option, but in this situation, I did; and as we settled into bed together, I realized that it was in that simple choice where I changed the trajectory of our evening from arguing to joy as I snuggled up to my man.

It's always a choice, and usually the choice hinges on something simple like forgiveness or making your spouse pay. Proving how right you are or extending grace. Not easy, but it is a choice, and our choices have consequences.

How are you handling the simple choices in your marriage? Are you extending mercy or slamming the dagger deeper into your spouse's heart? Choose wisely. These choices add up and make a marriage fulfilling, or they slowly erode and destroy.

More Romance Killers

"Ughhh, would you stop that!" I brushed my husband's hand away from his foot.

"Sorry," he replied with a smirk. "I didn't realize I was doing it."

I sighed.

Most evenings, we would snuggle together and watch our favorite shows, and every night, about thirty or so minutes in, I would hear—*pick, pick, pick.*

And I would look over and see my husband picking his toenails and flinging them upon the floor.

Gross factor big time.

"I don't know why it's such a big deal," he sheepishly commented.

"It just is," I replied. "It grates my nerves, and truth be told, it doesn't set us up for any intimate activities if that's what you're after."

"Well, I'm not tonight," he grinned.

"Still, it doesn't help with your future chances," I replied. "Especially as I'm stepping on your big nasty toenail remains when I get out of bed the next morning."

"Oh, give me a break," he laughed. "Have you looked at the bottom of your feet lately? My toenail remains are the least of your concern!"

He was referring to the fact that I usually walk around barefoot throughout our house (and yard and driveway), and this habit leads to some pretty filthy feet at the end of the day. Maybe you think I'm a horrible housecleaner and should do a better job of keeping my floors clean—which is not high on my priority list—but the filth on our floors derives more from our children who track in dirt, and that dirt usually shows up on the bottom of my feet.

The dirt on my feet really doesn't bother me, and I will reference the health benefits of grounding to anyone who will listen, but my husband is a different story. He visibly gags if we are lounging together on the couch—in the pitch-dark mind you because that's how Ryan lives, like a cave man saving all the energy all the time—and I attempt to put my feet on his lap.

And then, as we watch television together, he commentates, another huge romance killer! Every word the newscaster speaks, my husband thinks is being spoken directly to him—magically through the air waves! And he expects me to also partake in the conversation when all I want to do is sit peacefully and listen.

Newscaster—"Blah, Blah, Blah."

Ryan, "What?! That's ridiculous. I can't believe that's even a thing! Honey—" looking directly at me as I'm reading a book. "Honey, did you hear what he said? Can you believe it?"

I slap my book down on the coffee table. "Ryan Ronne, I love you, but I don't want to talk to the TV. I also don't want to talk to you while you're talking to the TV. I'd simply like to enjoy my book right now, if that's okay? Feel free to chat with the newscaster, but leave me out of the conversation."

Toenails, dirty feet, lights out, and talking to the TV—oh, and the messy counters in the bathroom that drive my husband batty. These are the Ronne hills. Do we die on these hills or buy a new pair of shoes? A pair of shoes that might perhaps be better equipped to handle these treacherous paths? That's the million-dollar question.

We haven't purchased new shoes but have instead learned to navigate these terrains, not that it changes much. We are both aware of the other's annoying quirks, and eleven years into marriage, we have chosen to, for the most part, live with them. Ryan still talks to the newscasters, and I've learned to tolerate this quirk.

He's also learned that I am not going to wear shoes in the house. I'm just not. I am a woman who walks around with my dirty bare feet. I do wash them before bed, which seems to be a compromise we have settled on.

What quirks do you see in your spouse that cause your blood pressure to rise a bit? It might be time to ask yourself, is this really a big deal? Does it warrant a conversation, or can I learn to live with it? Some things are a big deal. I know that when we move out of our temporary home, I don't want my bathroom counters to resemble what we currently have going on; but due to a limited amount of space, it is what it is. Take inventory, have the conversations if need be, and then accept your spouse in all their ridiculous quirkiness.

7

SPIRITUALITY

Growing Faith Contributes to a Growing Marriage

We've made it to the end of our HIS and HERS acronym, and now we will explore the spiritual component of a relationship. Ryan and I started our marriage with a strong foundation of faith. We were raised in Christian homes where church attendance was expected and served as a comforting community during our times of crisis. We continued this faith pattern and discovered that the best way for us to stay united was to daily submit our lives through prayer. Often these prayers hold an immense amount of depth as we cry out for answers, and sometimes, they are hurried and to the point: *Lord, you know our list of concerns. Go before us and open or close doors according to your sovereign will.* Most of the time, the prayers probably sound monotonous as we bring the same laundry list of requests: keep our family healthy, help our children make wise decisions, protect us as we move forward on x, y, or z, and guide us as we attempt this or that.

The point of prayer isn't that God needs us to pray. It's not a magical potion. It is about submitting our will to a higher power and recognizing that he is God and we are not, and that is that. I resonate with Job's wisdom: "The LORD gave, and the LORD has taken away; blessed be the name of the LORD" (Job 1:21 ESV). It is not our job to figure it out. It is instead our job to walk in radical obedience to what he has called us to endure. When questioned about the importance of my faith, I offer this simple explanation: I'd rather live my life through a lens of faith than fear. I'd rather believe that there is more beyond the here and now and that this life of pain and hardship and toiling under the sun isn't the end when we die but instead only the beginning. I have faith that when we run our race with perseverance, we are rewarded through our Savior's coveted words, "Well done, good and faithful servant" (Matt. 25:23). I would rather believe this—even if it's the biggest hoax that's ever been played on humanity. I would rather believe and live my life in such a way as to gain this reward than live my life without hope. Hope is what drives the human race and gets me out of bed in the morning. Hope that there is more than what meets the eye. Part of running my race is honoring the vows I took in my first marriage: to love, honor, and cherish until death do us part, and Jason and I were put through the wringer between his and Lucas's health struggles. Now, with my remarriage to Ryan, running my race includes honoring the vows I've taken once again: vows to love, honor, and cherish this sinful human being with baggage that quite honestly drives me crazy at times. He vowed the same with his sinful, quirky, opinionated wife! We believe in the spiritual nature of our union and in holding on when times are tough. We believe in forgiving one another—often. We believe that blessing follows obedience—especially obedience to our marital vows, and we claim favor over our blended family for generations to come. Amen.

The Two Become One

Ryan and I figured we were pros at this thing called marriage. We had experienced successful loving relationships the first time around, and those relationships were drenched in massively trying times including cancer, newborn babies, and special needs. We assumed this second journey of love would be a piece of cake, right? A spouse is a spouse is a spouse, or so we told ourselves. Never mind that the subs coming in had completely different personalities and desires than the ones who had left. Long story short, our naivete lasted about a whole sixty seconds after we said "I do."

We were midflight on our way to a desperately needed honeymoon in Cancún, Mexico, after our official wedding at the church. The weeks leading up to the big day had been stressful with seven young children, and finally, we were on our way to sunny Mexico where we would bask in our love for one another morning, noon, and night without a care in the world. Except that's not exactly what occurred.

We arrived, went through customs, and settled into our room. After surveying the goodies in the honeymoon basket left in our boudoir, I opened a cool, crisp mineral water from our private stash, and we walked down the meandering path and headed in the direction of a highly rated French cuisine restaurant.

We both ordered the filet mignon, which was glorious, as well as the flourless chocolate cake and champagne, and as we rubbed our stuffed bellies, we strolled toward a relaxing area on the beach lined with private cabanas. We requested a drink from the bartender and settled in under the stars. I gently laid my head on Ryan's chest, overwhelmed with love and gratitude that the Lord had redeemed my story so beautifully with this new man I was blessed to call my husband.

"I am so happy being here with you right now," I whispered to him as I gazed up at the starry night and then continued. "Jason had too much energy to ever sit still for long, so it's nice to have a husband who can relax." And in an instant, that innocent comment opened a huge can of worms.

Why in the world I thought it would be appropriate to compare my new husband to my late husband on the first night of our honeymoon, I have no idea; but in offering that second sentence, I offered a crack in what should have been a firm boundary. It wasn't so much that those words were the problem but that those words opened a door for a conversation about "them." Within five minutes, "they" became our entire focus for the next hour, and not so much in a healthy, memorable type of way but more in a mudslinging, comparison type of way.

"She would have never said that!"

"Well, he would have never acted like that!"

"Well! Well! Well!"

You get the point.

Nice way to end our first romantic evening together on our honeymoon, right?

Lord, have mercy.

We have come a long way since that cringeworthy moment, but sadly "they" continued to come up regularly in conversations during those first years of marriage. "They" continued to pop up in our relationship because we had not taken our time and grieved the end of those relationships properly, nor did we entirely grasp the covenantal aspect of our marriage vows, which were to "forsake all others and love, honor, and cherish this one individual." Not this individual plus the one I used to be married to.

I'm not saying there's anything wrong with their names being brought up in conversation; however, because we were so new in our love for one another and because our previous history had been spent with this other person and because Ryan and I had moved quickly in getting married when maybe we should have gotten therapy, we were still dealing with ghosts of the past. We had not entirely embraced the concept of the "two becoming one," and instead we allowed these previous spouses an unhealthy place in our covenant relationship.

It was what it was.

We have repented of our naive ways and asked for forgiveness from one another, and today, with eleven years of history and having raised a family, had a baby, and moved four times, we now have a shared history. We've learned that there are boundaries that belong in a marriage—especially when the ghosts of the past may cause pain to the one present, the one for whom we did vow to "forsake all others."

When we constantly drudged up the past and the comparisons these conversations often led to, including sainted memories of our previous spouses, we were not honoring our vows. The two shall become one means exactly what it says. I choose you as my spouse. I choose to love, honor, and cherish you. I choose to set aside the active love I had for a previous spouse and pour that love, energy, and devotion into you because we are now one—not you and me plus them.

It's tricky, but I've witnessed too many marriages with widowed spouses where the current spouse does not feel loved, honored, or cherished but feels like a backup plan—like plan B. That's no way to have a successful relationship.

We grew from the experience. We talked, pursued therapy, and learned.

One of my absolute favorite things on my honeymoon was the flourless chocolate cake at the French restaurant. I've managed to recreate a version of it for us to enjoy at home too.

Flourless Chocolate Cake with Homemade Whipped Cream

- 1 cup dark chocolate chips
- 8 Tbsp butter
- 3/4 cup sugar
- 1/4 tsp salt
- 1 tsp vanilla
- 3 eggs
- 1/2 cup cocoa powder
- 1/2 cup maple syrup
- 8 oz whipping cream

Preheat the oven to 375° F. Lightly grease a metal 8" round cake pan. Put the chocolate and butter in a nonstick pot over low heat. Stir constantly until melted. Transfer to a mixing bowl, and stir in the sugar, salt, and vanilla. Add the eggs, beating briefly until smooth. Add the cocoa powder, and mix just to combine. Spoon the batter into the prepared pan. Bake for 25 minutes; the top will have formed a thin crust. Remove it from the oven, and let it cool it in the pan for 5 minutes.

Whipped Cream

Place the whipping cream and maple syrup in a bowl with a stand mixer and beat until soft peaks appear. Place a dollop of whipped cream on each slice of cake.

Building Our House on the Rock

As I write this chapter, we are approximately one hundred days away from moving into our new house. Also, as I write this chapter, the world is going through some heavy stuff. There are divisions across our nation that seem to be birthed out of social media as our fears drive us deeper into despair, and we devour whatever we can find that seems to be newsworthy. The problem is our brains aren't meant to handle the sheer amount of information we accumulate on a daily basis. This fear-based paranoia has led to numerous divisions, and the more our world slips away from our godly heritage, the more I lean into what the Bible has to say.

I was recently driving to my office, thinking about the heaviness within the world as I listened to a popular podcast. This podcast had become my mommy treat most days, but on this day, it felt heavy. The military had recently pulled out of Afghanistan, and there were angry opinions about how the mission had been mishandled. As I listened, I didn't feel a peace from knowing more. No, I felt more despair and anger and wondered how my children were supposed to grow up in this world. How could I raise them in a world that seemed hell-bent on teaching them anything but the truth? It was heavy, and I didn't have answers. I turned the podcast off even though it was usually a source of joy and turned on my favorite Christian radio station.

The song "The Blessing" by Kari Jobe blasted through the airways.

As the words saturated the car and drenched my weary soul, I found myself sobbing, sobbing in agreement with the words, and I began to claim them over my family:

> May His favor be upon you
> And a thousand generations
> And your family and your children
> And their children, and their children

My deepest desire for my family is that one day, when I'm old and gray, Ryan and I will look back on our legacy and see our children and their children and their children's children, and we will see a godly heritage, a family bent toward Heaven. As the tears streamed down my face, I knew we had work to do at our new build site.

That evening, I brought up my idea at family devotion time.

"I think we should write our favorite Bible verses on the new house."

"What do you mean?" asked Josh.

"We should each pick a verse to claim for our life and write it on the boards in our new house," I clarified.

"Ohhhhh," he replied.

"And that way," I continued, "we can invite God's presence into our lives and claim his promises over our family."

The crew agreed, and we set to work picking out our favorite verses. The next week we headed to our new house for "church," where we spent the hour penning Scripture over our house and claiming the Lord's promises for our family. When the job was completed, we ventured back home to rest, where I plugged my shuffle into the computer and purchased my new favorite tune: "The Blessing," which I now walk to every day and claim over my family.

What is your family struggling with? What promises from the Word do you need to speak or write over your situation? Commit to praying these promises over the next days and weeks, and then step back and let the Lord do his work.

Holding on When Times Get Tough

One hot and sticky summer night, I rummaged through our attic and came across an old calendar from 2010. I gingerly flipped through the pages and paused when I arrived at August, the most difficult month of my life. A tumultuous month jam-packed with overwhelming obligations and demands: work, Lucas's birthday, family pictures, doctor's appointments, four children farmed out on a daily basis to anyone and everyone, the arrival of hospice equipment, nursing staff coming and going, important phone calls to make life or death decisions, and ultimately, goodbyes whispered and a funeral prepared for a young husband and father.

Today, eleven years later, I bask in the warmth of the sun, a beautiful fall day spent watching my rambunctious daughter fill her little red wagon with dry autumn leaves as I hang freshly laundered clothing on the line. A day I could not have imagined in my wildest dreams in August of 2010. A day seeping with redemption, warmth, and joy.

The moral of the story? Circumstances can change in an instant. In 2010, I found myself in the midst of an unimaginable hell as my husband prepared to leave earth for Heaven, and I prepared for what life would hold as a single mom of four young children. The experience was unbelievably exhausting and one of the most challenging times I've been called to faithfully endure; but hear this truth. I held on with every ounce of my being. I held on to him who is greater than he who is in the world. I held on to that last shred of faith in my soul no matter how unraveled or mangled or beat to crap it seemed to be in that moment. I held on for goodness' sake, and for every other sake in the world because I had no idea what was around the bend, but I knew that he is faithful, and he would redeem my story.

I met Ryan a few months later, and the rest is history. No, it hasn't always been easy (as you can read about in my books!), but there has been redemption. My ashes have been traded in for beauty: a beautiful life full of children and special needs and responsibilities and pain and joy. There is fullness in redemption— fullness of his faithfulness and his grace.

And you also, dear reader, have no idea what may be in store for you when the Almighty flips your page. You have no idea the blessing he may bestow when you "fight the good fight and finish the race." Hold the course. Stay faithful in your marriage. Stay faithful to your family. Be obedient and take the next right step forward. You will have your peace again; you will have your joy. You will rise and have the crown of life bestowed upon your weary head; and you will hear those coveted words: "Well done, good and faithful servant." I promise, your faithfulness will win in this life or the next.

> Blessed is the one who perseveres under trial because, having stood the test, that person will receive the crown of life that the Lord has promised to those who love him. (James 1:12)

Staying Grounded

Over the past few years, I've witnessed the demise of many leaders, often pinnacles of faith who have fallen from grace; men and women who most assuredly began their careers with the noblest of intentions. Individuals who, through the passage of time, became enamored with self and blinded by fame and fortune; people who lost perspective on their place within humanity because of a choice to turn from that still small voice, and who, more often than not, walked away from their marriage vows because of pride.

I believe we each have the innate potential to fall far from grace, to perceive ourselves as better than we ought to, and this perception can often lead to betrayal or divorce. Under different circumstances, I could really embrace how special I think I am, hold on tightly to the perception that I've gotten this life thing figured out, lean into pride and her enticing offers, and allow her to nibble away at my soul as she has with others who have climbed the ladder of success.

I think about all this as I write books and produce documentaries about the challenges caregivers face and run a nonprofit. All projects that could potentially cast a bright light on my life.

Perhaps.

I'm a firstborn, "I can do it," Enneagram One who thrives on making a difference in the world, and these attributes are typically celebrated by society with accolades and praise; and yes, this recognition is nice. It's nice to be acknowledged for your achievements and even nicer still to have people perceive you as a good person; a person making positive strides in the steps of humanity.

Of course, it's nice.

I've worked diligently and finished projects that might push me a little bit out of the shadows of anonymity and possibly into a world for which I am unprepared and yet—

I will continue to rise every morning
And care for my brood of children
Five teenagers currently
And one with profound disabilities.

I will continue to bathe my seventeen-year-old son
(which is as humility building as it gets some days)
And help him get dressed
And pour his juice into a sippy cup
And put socks on his feet
And lace up his sneakers
And assist him to the car
And gently close the door, but not until he says in his sweet singsong way,
"Bye! Have a good day!"
And I turn and walk away
With a smile on my face.
This is my routine
Every single day.

These monotonous actions serve as a reminder, as they did for the apostle Paul—a prickly thorn that breathes humility into my swelling soul and deflates any pride that may try to sneak in, crushing it in an instant as my miracle boy demands yet another round of, *Paddy cake, paddy cake, baker's man, bake me a cake as fast as you can.*

And as his smile reaches for the stars, I lean into the understanding that he and I are created in the image of our Maker. One not better than the other, simply different with unique purposes and gifts, and the only attribute that makes us great is dutifully reacting in joyful obedience to the hard and holy tasks we've been called to accomplish. Each staying faithful to the race we must run.

This uncomfortable road, this thorn of special needs, this aching joy serves as a gift—a gift that calls me to daily lay down my life and continuously keeps my head from ballooning and serves as a constant jab reminding me of who I am and who I am not by stripping away any pretenses. This gift keeps me grounded in my marriage and daily returns me to the one I love rather than seeking affirmation in the arms of another man. This gift prepares a table before me in the presence of fame and fortune and pride; where Lucas and I dine with the Shepherd, feasting on humility and special needs and gulping down goblets of grace.

It is well with my soul.

It is well with Lucas's soul.

And that is enough.

These seemingly mundane tasks are the ones the Lord smiles upon—these monotonous tasks that seem insignificant in the grand scheme of life. These are holy tasks; serving our families, caring for those who cannot care for themselves, making dinner and cleaning toilets and folding laundry—the "feet washing" tasks of the world. And the irony is that these are the tasks that make us worthy in the eyes of our Maker.

What tasks do you need to reframe in the light of holy obedience? Folding laundry? Getting groceries? Helping kids with homework? Pray that the Lord helps you reframe these monotonous tasks in light of eternity.

Lay It on the Closet Floor

"Honey, can I come in?" he pleaded from the other side of the bathroom wall. "Let's talk this through. I don't want you to hurt alone. You need to find a way to truly forgive me so we can move forward in our marriage."

"Okay," I barely whispered.

He let himself into the bathroom and slowly headed to the closet. That's where he found me, curled in a fetal position on the floor, tears streaming down my face as I dealt with "the issue" yet again. The issue that refused to die in my mind. The pornography issue laced in distrust, lies, and insecurities.

The lying and partial truths did as much damage as the original sexual sin had. Even after I received the truth, I struggled with trusting Ryan, and the pain the lies caused has reemerged on occasion in the heat of an argument. It was in these moments when Ryan found me crumpled on the closet floor, yet again, as the memories flooded my mind, and my heart grew hardened toward my husband. Complete forgiveness was a long process, but it slowly arrived as I extended grace by repeatedly refusing to see the sin but to instead see the sinner, my husband, a fallen human in need of a Savior, just like myself. Once we were on an equal playing field, both in need of grace, I could no longer withhold the forgiveness he so desperately needed.

Ryan's Take

When I think back on these times, it saddens me greatly. I never intended to hurt my wife through my insecurities and what seemed like personal problems that were none of her business. They were none of her business . . . until she considered marrying me. That's when the "in good times and bad" and "the two shall become one" really took effect. I wasn't honoring the vows I swore to Jess. Some of you, including many of my extended family, will consider pornography just a part of a man's life. I would agree that in our world it has become a very normal occurrence, but this doesn't make it okay.

I felt a lot of guilt for what I brought into our marriage; but more than that was the guilt I felt because of how often I was forced to lie to protect my secret life. Admitting it to Jess was one of the hardest things I've ever had to do, but once I revealed that part of my life to her, I felt a weight lift; and over time, Jess forgave me. Statistics show that over 90 percent of men have struggled with pornography at some point in their life, and I hope that my vulnerability will encourage the hard conversations needed in many marriages.

I pray that Jess can be an inspiration to the wives who are forced to face this reality and do their best to forgive. No man wants pornography and lust to rule his life, and deep down he wants to be honest with those he loves. It is an agonizing process; but if we can get through it, so can you.

Jess, I am so sorry for the pain my sin has caused. Thank you for forgiving me and extending grace when everything in you said to run. Thank you for not giving up on me and for continuing to encourage me to be the best version of myself. I would have never faced this problem and for sure would have never overcome it without you.

TAKEAWAYS

FOR LEARNING HOW TO FORGIVE

- Understand that the process will take time—and that includes getting to a point of complete forgiveness.
- Both spouses must be completely vulnerable during the process and allow for transparency and honesty.
- You both must be 100 percent committed to healing your marriage.
- Start praying together every morning if you don't already. As a wife, it is extremely helpful for me to hear my husband cry out to the Lord for strength, and it softens my heart toward his struggles.
- Find a trusted friend or therapist to help maneuver your way through the pain.

True Faith?

I struggled to believe Ryan was a true Christian after his battle with pornography was revealed. As someone who sees the world through a black-and-white lens, I perceive things to be right or wrong, and I couldn't rationalize how a man of faith could repeatedly betray his wives sexually, lie about it, and call himself a believer. I understood sin and repentance and attempting to change, but I didn't see how years of struggling with a particular sin could coexist with faith. I was concerned that Ryan was playing Christian rather than being a Christian. Playing Christian to appease those around him and, specifically, playing the role of a faithful husband to avoid my wrath. I didn't blame him. I wouldn't want my wrath either.

A few days after his confession, I was puttering about the kitchen. He had left early that morning to tear down an old barn, and I wrestled with feelings of betrayal and stupidity. I began to dwell on numerous situations where I wondered if Ryan had struggled with pornography, situations where I wasn't around or where he had acted "off" or more quiet than usual. My mind began to get the best of me as I dwelled on these scenarios, playing each one around in my mind, like a game of cat and mouse, wondering, *Was he struggling with pornography when we were dating? How far into our marriage? When, where, how, and why?* The obsessive nature took hold of my heart, and when he arrived home, I tentatively asked how his day had been. We were in a weird spot since the confession. A spot of tiptoeing around one another and not feeling safe in the relationship. I'm pretty sure it was a spot where Ryan felt split wide open in vulnerability.

"It was good," he smiled and then continued. "Although the Devil sure knew how to play my strings today."

"Why?" I questioned, somewhat afraid of what the answer held.

"Well," he sighed, "as I was tearing down the barn, I came across some old *Playboy* magazines, and my first instinct was to not tell you and hide them, but I didn't."

I held my breath, afraid to ask how he proceeded.

"I didn't," he said. "And instead I brought them home to burn, and I want you to be with me when I do it because I think I need accountability." He continued, "I promise to bring you into every temptation that comes my way if you promise to hold me accountable, not yell at me, and pray me through."

I sighed. If I'm honest, I wish I could have 100 percent believed what he was saying, but we were still a long way from this reality. Outwardly, I nodded my head yes. I would support Ryan in this endeavor. But inwardly, I wondered if he had hidden a few of the magazines for later; if he was admitting a partial truth to appease me and then would do what he wanted to do.

Later that night, we started a fire and threw the magazines into it; and as we stood there together, hand in hand, the Lord spoke to my heart: "Let any one of you who is without sin be the first to throw a stone" (John 8:7).

Who was I to question someone's faith? I certainly was not without sin. I sinned with my mouth all the time, getting angry at my husband or others whom I felt had done me wrong rather than making every attempt to live in peace. I gossiped about people. I slandered and spewed in my worst moments. I certainly was not blameless, and yet the Lord continued to provide mercy, and in his abundant grace, I learned, ever so slowly, to rest and find my worth in him, which is exactly what my husband needed from me. My distrust would not change Ryan and would only send him further into isolation, which would not be helpful in his battle with pornography. The best thing I could do was offer him a fresh start—a graceful start—just like my Savior offered me on a daily basis.

I turned to my husband and gave him a hug. "We'll get through this," I promised. "I love you, and I promise to help you without hurting you."

"Deal," he whispered as we walked back inside.

I can't be the only wife who has felt doubt as her spouse confessed sin. Even as we burned those magazines, we were a long way off from complete restoration and trust. My mind did a number on me for months, even though Ryan offered complete transparency and the ability to ask at any point, "Hey, how are you doing?"

And I asked often. Now, I can't remember the last time I asked because I haven't seen any signs that would indicate that there's a problem. This is one of those situations that simply took time. It took time to rebuild trust. It took time to rebuild intimacy. It took time for the forgiveness I offered to really feel authentic. But we got there, and so can you.

Till Death Do Us Part

Our oldest daughter, Mya, recently said to me, "I bet you and Dad are one of those couples who dies within hours of each other."

I looked up from the book I was reading, slightly surprised. "Oh yeah?" I questioned. "Why do you say that?"

"Because it seems like you have such a deep love that you probably wouldn't make it long without the other one."

I smiled, happy that she made that observation at such a young age. Ryan and I come from broken homes, and we have a desire to give our children the gift of an intact, happy, healthy, and thriving family as they age. We understand that the younger years with our children were/are chaotic, and at times we feel like we are simply in survival mode, but we see a light at the end of the tunnel, a light as the kids age and set off into the world to carve out lives for themselves. We envision them coming home one day, to their parents and siblings, and this gift of an intact family is one we strive to give them by prioritizing our marriage now.

Healthy marriages are an integral part of a stable society. Often, a good marital relationship leads to healthy families; from healthy families come emotionally stable, healthy children; from those children, another generation of healthy marriages; and the cycle continues, God willing. Proverbs 27:17—"As iron sharpens iron, so one person sharpens another"—is a good analogy for any marriage. We draw out each other's weaknesses, in a good way. We shouldn't pretend they don't exist. Instead, we call attention to them, and we get to the heart of what they are about. We pray about these struggles and become strengthened through the practice of honesty with one another.

Our kids see our commitment to each other and get excited when their favorite babysitter comes over to spoil them while Mom and Dad go out. They giggle and hide their eyes when Daddy brushes up on Mom and sneaks a kiss, and Mom swats his hand off her behind and tells him to "stop." This is the example we strive to set—the excitement they witness as we get ready to have some alone time without them. They benefit, and we benefit.

Someday I want our kids to take with them a picture of a fun marriage, a marriage in which Mom and Dad make each other a top priority. They are being trained to live independent from us for most of their lives; however, my husband is the "till death do you part" piece of the equation, and by cultivating this relationship, the rest will hopefully fall into place much easier.

Codependent or Dependent on the Lord?

The Hebrew word "*ezer*," which appears in the Old Testament twenty-one times, is a complex and difficult word to translate. I used to cringe when I heard pastors talk about how it meant that a wife was supposed to be a helpmate or helper to her husband. *Of course*, I thought, *it always goes back to the man; the chauvinistic male ego that the godly woman is forever upholding.* After a deeper dive into what this word means, I was pleasantly surprised to discover that it may have been taken out of context, and a more accurate translation would include a twofold meaning: to rescue / to save and to be strong.

When Ryan and I dated, he wrote me a beautiful book about how I had served as his princess in shining armor by coming alongside him in life and offering my strength. Ryan was in the depths of despair when I met him. His wife had just died from brain cancer, and he was a young widower with three children. His journey had been abrupt and fast whereas my journey had lasted three years; by the time Jason passed away, I had gone through the stages of grief and had reached a point of acceptance. Shortly after Ryan and I got married, we went to therapy to deal with some issues that arose out of our new life together. Therapy is where we uncovered that he and I have a bit of a codependency issue within our marriage. I'm not sure we could have *not* had this issue after the trauma and PTSD we lived with for so long. The codependency would manifest in massive anxiety issues when Ryan had to leave town; and if one of us became sick, even with something like the flu, the other spouse would often be sent into a panic as we relived what we had gone through with our first spouses. We owned this codependency, and it has lessened as we've had to get comfortable being apart for periods of time.

I've considered this diagnosis over our marriage. A diagnosis with a negative connotation. No one wants to be labeled codependent. That word implies neediness, and no one wants to be perceived as needy; but as I've thought about it, I've changed my perspective. Ryan and I are very much dependent on one another in this life we've created with our children. Everything in our life must adhere to the rhythms we've instilled, rhythms that work well in our busy lives. Routines needed for Lucas to receive the therapies and resources he needs. Routines abided by so we can make a living and pay our bills. The Ronnes have these rhythms that make our lives, and yes, there is an aspect of codependency within these routines. I need Ryan to do what he says he's going to do, and he requires the same from me. There's not a lot of wiggle room, and that does make us dependent on the other to live up to their expectations.

For example, from time to time as the pressure mounts, I've thought about running away from home. Not always but sometimes. Getting in my car and driving straight to Florida. I'm sure Ryan has had similar feelings, but the complexity of our life together has saved us from leaving. Even saved us from divorce in the early years! Loyalty, rhythms, and time have ironed out many of the issues that once seemed insurmountable. Neither of us wants to raise eight children alone or do special needs alone or add the stress of coparenting every other week, and so we have stayed married—out of love, respect, convenience, and a level of codependency. By staying married, we have grown a deep and abiding love for one another that maybe we would have given up on years ago if our circumstances had been different, maybe easier circumstances that included two or three children and no special needs. But our situation made it almost impossible to even entertain those thoughts. Sure, my brash mouth threatened divorce a time or two when life felt like it was spinning out of control and my gut reaction was to walk away, but when I thought about what that scenario realistically would look like, it didn't look any easier! In fact, it looked a heck of a lot harder without a partner, and so I sat my behind down and instead of running away, Ryan and I worked through our problems. We had to! The alternative looked like doing our complicated life alone without the support and love of another person. That didn't seem like fun at all.

TAKEAWAY

The term "codependency" can be reframed in light of our spiritual union with our spouse to be a positive thing that not only keeps us married but keeps us growing in love and respect for one another.

Radical Obedience

Therefore, my beloved, as you have always obeyed, so now, not only as in my presence but much more in my absence, work out your own salvation with fear and trembling, for it is God who works in you, both to will and to work for his good pleasure. (Phil. 2:12–13 ESV)

What does it mean to work out our salvation?

What determines faith? Or godliness? A man or woman wholeheartedly committed to the Lord? What is the "it" factor that David possessed, a man after God's own heart? Or Enoch, who "walked with God and then was no more"? Or Mary, supernaturally impregnated, holding the Messiah within her womb? Noah, who was credited with blamelessness?

The more I meditate on the actions of these heroes of faith, the more I see how everything is connected to obedience—actions intertwined with movement forward—and obedience becomes the barometer of faithfulness and even surpasses character flaws, personality quirks, and bad choices. And this obedience is often required in the face of a seemingly ridiculous request, a request that the rest of the world might find unbelievable and absurd, a request that quite likely will require brash courage and thick skin because the naysayers will have some naysaying for sure. A request that might look like two crazy thirty-three-year-olds falling in love only months after their spouses died and marrying one another to create a big, crazy, chaotic life with eight children.

I've been asked to obey ridiculous requests a time or two: Carry a terminal baby and then raise him by laying down my desire for easy every single day for seventeen plus years, and obey what I've been called to do—care for a child who cannot care for one single need without assistance. I obeyed and married a widower, a man with three young children, less than a year after burying my husband. I obeyed and became a voice for caregivers, and I've told my story, including the really hard parts, despite a spirit of fear. And I started a nonprofit even though it was and still is a ton of volunteer work.

I've been ridiculed, mocked, and questioned. Heck, I've questioned myself a time or two. My resolve has wavered, but there's been a protection of grace, which arises out of obedience:

obedience in spite of my stubbornness, mouthiness, know-it-all attitude, grumbling, and, at times, bad choices.

Sometimes I joyfully obey, and sometimes I do not. Sometimes I make good choices, and sometimes I do not. Sometimes I obey immediately, and sometimes it takes weeks or months; but I believe my heart is measured not by my human reactions and tendencies, but instead by the level of obedience I extend to the difficult calls that have been placed on my life.

Every action is either obedience toward his perfect will or disobedience to what he's called me to do.

And the working out part?

That's where (hopefully) the character flaws and personality quirks and bad choices start to iron out. Instead of grumbling, I zip it. Instead of whining and complaining at my spouse, I speak kindly. Instead of zoning out on Facebook, maybe I enjoy a date night with my husband. Choice by choice, moment by moment in obedience, I am called to walk toward his ultimate purpose and plan.

And that, friends, is where the sweet spot is found. That place of peace and rest—even in the middle of the most chaotic of lives.

Stay beside the Shepherd. Continue to move forward in obedience to the calling on your marriage and your family. That is where the blessing will be found along with heaps of grace, mercy, and forgiveness. This is where the Shepherd will sustain you.

Stay strong friends. He will provide.

Fear or Faith

I recently enjoyed a lovely conversation with a mama of a twenty-year-old total-care daughter. As we chatted, I was reminded that my Lucas will turn eighteen this summer, and as of now, we don't have a long-term plan. Sure, I have aspirations and dreams, but nothing is cemented in stone, and this leads to numerous fears about what his future holds. And what my future looks like.

And these fears are amplified when Lucas's aggression intensifies. He recently lashed out at me. He wasn't trying to be mean or abusive, but he reacted when I tried to put his shoes on. He didn't want to go anywhere, and his response was to scratch me and pull my hair. He's seventeen years old, and I often wonder how much longer I'll have the strength to do this. When you live in constant fight-or-flight mode, you use adrenaline surges to your advantage, but I'm not sure how much longer I can physically care for him without major repercussions when he doesn't get his way.

So instead of being a sane individual and prepping for a move or writing a book I'm under contract for or meal planning or any of the many tasks I must accomplish, I spent the day obsessively researching how to become a Medicaid provider and start a residential facility.

I looked at vacant land, at huge pole barn kits that could be sectioned off into living quarters, duplexes, cheap commercial properties that my handy husband could renovate, and then I crunched the numbers, which only resulted in disappointing results. It's a hefty price tag to have your loved one cared for 24/7.

My point is this: as many of you prepare to launch high school graduates off, full of anticipation and hope over a world of possibilities (which I'm doing as well with my two oldest), there are those of us freaking out about the future of our unique kiddos.

I believe most of my grief with Lucas has nothing to do with his diagnosis but much more to do with the uncertainty of his future and ours. If someone were to say to me, "At twenty-two years old, he will move into this amazing residential facility where he will be well loved and cared for," that would work! But no one says this to parents like me. We don't hold our breath for admittance to college at eighteen years old. We don't hold our breath for admittance to anything! No, we hold our breath that there will be an opening somewhere that provides peace to our souls before our child turns forty or before we die. Whatever comes first.

We live for years in fear over what the future holds; and I, for one, am sick of the fear. So in true Jessica fashion, I decided to take the bull by the horns and try to control the situation.

After my chat with this woman, I decided to go for a walk to decompress and work through some of the fear, and these thoughts swirled about:

How do I continue to care for someone who might hurt me? When he's stronger than I am and can really make his desires known if he wants to? What does our future look like? What are our options if nothing opens up? How will this affect my marriage? Or my ability to help with my grandchildren someday?

And then the tears seeped out of the corners of my eyes because this was my baby boy I was contemplating—the child I was told would never live—and lately my deep desire to keep him safe has been overridden with despair and fear: not a place where I like to camp out.

Not a place I enjoy at all.

As I considered these thoughts, a still, small voice whispered, *Don't doubt in the dark what I showed you in the light.*

I've always had faith that God would provide. I've always had faith that there would be a safe place for Lucas when the time arrived to release him into the world. I've had faith, but lately my faith sounds more like that of a doubting Thomas.

Don't doubt in the dark what I showed you in the light.

Dear faithful mama, place your hand in my side. Feel the agony I suffered at Calvary. Know how much I love you and Lucas. I will care for him. I will care for you, and I will provide in due time. In my time. My grace is sufficient for this moment. Manna for each day but only for the day. Simply move forward in obedience.

It's hard to release the control of Lucas's future into the Lord's hands. You would think I would be an expert by now after living in the Lord's faithfulness, but I'm not and need constant reminders that he will provide in his time.

What do you need to release control of today? What fear is keeping you in bondage? Release it, and rest in the knowledge that he goes before you. He knows your situation and holds you in the palm of his hand.

So don't be afraid; you are worth more than many sparrows. (Matt. 10:31)

BATH SPRINGS

I want to share a cool story of faith as I close out this book, and I hope it brings hope to your weary heart. I've talked about how we purchased what we thought was our dream house in rural Tennessee, a big sprawling home that we poured our hearts into for seven years. We renovated the entire dwelling and made it our own. We planted gardens and danced in the rain when the pipes burst, our kids ate fried crickets, and we buried our unborn baby in the cemetery plot high on the hill. I walked the dusty driveway often, beseeching the Lord for answers, and sometimes I received clarity and sometimes I heard silence, but still I trusted that his will would be done.

In 2019, we moved from what we thought was our dream life to suburbia, outside of Nashville, to pursue more resources for Lucas. We put our big beautiful rural home on the market where it sat without any interest for two years. Frustrated about the lack of interest, Ryan decided to view this property as a flip house and traveled back and forth throughout the weeks completing the unfinished projects in hopes that it would somehow finally sell—even for a low-ball offer. Still nothing. Nada, zip, zilch. People did not want to live that far out in rural America with a huge home in need of constant maintenance. Most people aren't as crazy as we are and aren't interested in the hardest project imaginable. Most people aren't the Ronnes.

Meanwhile, back in suburbia, we endured a global pandemic but still felt a lot of stress that there was zero movement on this house of ours. As we dreamed of moving to Michigan to build an accessible home for Lucas, we knew we had to unload this property in order to make room for our new dream. I was ready to take anything offered, and Ryan considered dropping the price over $100,000 and selling it to the only potential buyer we had encountered—a local businessman who liked a good deal and had plans to turn it into a lodge. We prayed and prayed and prayed. I felt desperate and beseeched Ryan to agree to sell it to this guy. He dropped the price by $50,000 on a Monday morning and said, "Jess, I don't have a peace about it selling it that low. Please be patient."

"Aghhhhh, Lord, open his heart!" I pleaded, my need to control the situation getting the best of me.

As I mentioned before, we attempted to sell this very unique house in the middle of a global pandemic. Attempted to sell this house in rural America. Attempted to sell this house when a vast majority of Americans were fleeing urban areas and desperately looking for a house in rural America, with Tennessee apparently being a favorite choice due to conservative values and low taxes. I tried to be patient.

We received a call Thursday night from our realtor—two years after listing this home. "You guys are not going to believe this, but there is a three-way bidding war on your house!"

"What?!" We were shocked. Apparently two New Yorkers and a local family were all desperate to move out to the middle of nowhere. "That's awesome!"

And then—another text a few hours later: "There's a fourth offer on the table!" Our realtor exclaimed, as shocked as we were.

After some quick negotiations, we were pleased to discover that all four offers were above asking price.

We prayed about it and felt a peace moving forward with one particular family; a family who has an autistic son. They desired a tranquil place with lots of land where he could be as loud as he wanted to; a family with whom the nonprofit I started, The Lucas Project, has talked about partnering. God is good. All the time.

And collectively, myself, my marriage, my family, you and yours, we continue to move forward in obedience, step by step, through the seasons of life: winter, spring, summer, and fall, each bringing their unique challenges and joys. We continue to move forward through joy, pain, triumph, and defeat. We move forward through the marital truths of His & Hers. We keep moving, somehow, toward life—for we must, right?

We just keep livin'.

Do you want to dive deeper into the HIS & HERS of your marriage? Join Jess and Ryan on a couple's journey with their study guide.

The seven-week study guide focuses on each main topic from this book: Health, Intimacy, Sex, Household tasks, Excitement, Romance, and Spirituality. This includes an extended look into the book with thoughtful questions and stimulating conversational starters. Also included each week are videos from Jess and Ryan to help further your study.

Get the free study guide now from

www.jessplusthemess.com
/lovin/studyguide!

1-877-816-4455 toll free
www.leafwoodpublishers.com

LEAFWOOD
PUBLISHERS
an imprint of Abilene Christian University Press

ALL THE DELICIOUS, CROWD-PLEASING RECIPES FOUND IN

LOVIN'
WITH
GRIT & GRACE

are available on beautiful recipe cards at
www.jessplusthemess.com/lovin/recipecards.

CHICKEN FRIED RICE

One of Ryan's favorite meals to make on his meal night is chicken fried rice, and the kids (and even Mom) love it too! Here's his tried-and-true recipe.

INGREDIENTS

3 large chicken breasts
1 package (12 oz) of mixed frozen vegetables
2 cups rice
Bone broth or water
8 large eggs, scrambled
1 stick of butter (8 Tbsp)
Soy sauce
Salt and pepper

METHOD

1. Make the rice with the bone broth or water according to the directions. Put aside.
2. Next, melt the butter in a skillet.
3. Add the chicken, salt and pepper both sides, and cook until the chicken is no longer pink.
4. Remove and cut into small pieces. Do not clean the skillet!
5. Add the eggs and scramble.
6. Add the rice, chicken, and vegetables.
7. Add salt, pepper, and soy sauce to taste.

You can print them for free and
add them to your family's favorite recipes.

BLENDED WITH GRIT AND GRACE

Just Keep Livin' When Life Is Unexpected

JESSICA RONNE

ISBN 978-1-68426-281-6

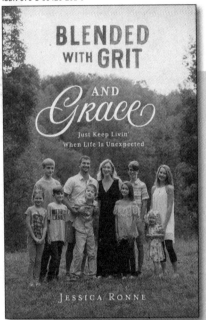

Life can be wonderful but also wacky and weary. You've just gotta keep livin.'

After losing their spouses to cancer in 2010, Jess and Ryan found each other and blended their families. This blending has led to an unexpected and often hilarious journey. *Blended with Grit and Grace* invites you to walk alongside them and learn what it's like to have eight kids under one roof.

With wit and wisdom, Jess offers fresh perspectives on managing different parenting styles, developing family traditions, and meeting the special needs of your family. Jess, with frequent asides from Ryan, also probes deeper marital and family concerns that are often experienced but not talked about, like grief, breakdowns in communication, finances, and insecurities. Filled with gentle advice, *Blended with Grit and Grace* transports you into the Ronne's kitchen so you can ponder the detours that have come up in your own life.

"This book is part memoir, part roadmap for spouses with blended families, part caregiving manual, and part cookbook. Prepare to laugh out loud while you read but have a tissue handy for when you're moved to tears."

—**JOLENE PHILO,** national speaker, coauthor (with Gary Chapman) of *Sharing Love Abundantly in Special Needs Families*

1-877-816-4455 toll free
www.leafwoodpublishers.com

an imprint of *Abilene Christian University Press*